HARRIETTE WILSON

Lady of Pleasure

Other books by Valerie Grosvenor Myer

Obstinate Heart: Jane Austen, a biography
Margaret Drabble: A Readers' Guide
Ten Great English Novelists
Culture Shock (a novel)
Charlotte Brontë: Truculent Spirit
Jane Austen
The Butterfly House (a novel)

Harriette Wilson

Lady of Pleasure

by

Valerie Grosvenor Myer

Fern House

First published in 1999 by
Fern House
High Street, Haddenham,
ELY, Cambridgeshire CB6 3XA

www.fernhouse.com

A catalogue record for this book is available
from the British Library

ISBN 0 9524897 9 1

Jacket by Chris Winch Design

Printed by TJ International Ltd, Padstow

CONTENTS

ACKNOWLEDGEMENTS

For valuable suggestions I am grateful to Paul Antill,
Nora Crook, Rodney Dale, Roy Palmer and, as always,
my husband Michael Grosvenor Myer.
Any errors are my own.

EPIGRAPH

On this soft anvil all the world is made.
— Rochester, *Sodom.*

Harriette, a 'smart, saucy girl, with good eyes and dark hair'

INTRODUCTION

by Sue Limb ('Dulcie Domum' of the *Guardian*)

I wish I had written this book, but as usual Valerie Grosvenor Myer has beaten me to it. Last time I envied a book of hers it was her sparkling biography of Jane Austen, the good girl of the Regency. Now she has turned her attention to the bad girl, Harriette Wilson.

I remember when I first heard of Harriette Wilson thirty years ago, it was like hearing gossip about a contemporary, not historical facts from the dusty archive of the past. Harriette Wilson was the Duke of Wellington's mistress and when she was planning to publish her memoirs and tried to blackmail him, he replied: 'Publish and be damned!' You never forget such anecdotes – even though, as Valerie Grosvenor Myer shows, that particular one is unlikely to be literally true.

But there are plenty of other hot and spicy anecdotes about Harriette, and they are served up here with a saucy relish. She wrote to the Prince of Wales, inviting him to have an affair with her; she always went to bed elegantly dressed in case she died in her sleep; she once got rid of a troublesome IOU by swallowing it. And she enjoyed an endless succession of lovers, from the pale, handsome foot-fetishist Ponsonby who haunted the parks accompanied by his Newfoundland dog, to Worcester, an Oxford undergraduate and the heir to the Beaufort estates, who became her adoring toyboy, and wanted to marry her, though his father the Duke bribed her to keep away.

Ponsonby and Worcester, along with most of her other lovers, were either already married when she met them or soon contracted prudent marriages to other, decent women, often heiresses. And beyond Harriette's insatiable progress through the breeches of the *beau monde* we can detect the 'debts and terrifying insecurity' which haunted her and her many similarly naughty sisters.

Indeed it seems that she only turned to blackmail in desperation, when her attractions were on the wane, influenced by the proximity of the debtors' prison and a husband who was a bad influence. Yes, she did finally marry, though paradoxically her spouse Rochfort plays an insignificant part in her emotional history. Nowadays he would probably be known as her publicist.

Her *Memoirs*, on which Valerie Grosvenor Myer has satisfyingly drawn, evoke a scintillating and sensational society. Provincial England may, as Jane Austen suggests, have been all proprieties, rookeries and rectories, but the

London over which Harriette Wilson triumphed was a hurly-burly of adultery, prize-fighting, wantonness and drunkenness. Harriette had her standards, however. She was always an elegant figure, dressed in white and wearing diamonds, and she insisted on 'respect' - one of many details which make her seem very vividly our contemporary.

Though her humble birth meant that to be a Lady of Pleasure was the only outlet for her personal magnetism, Harriette took full advantage of her sexual powers, not scrupling to manipulate her lovers, take bold initiatives to recruit new and distinguished admirers, and stand up to the most powerful figures in society if she found their conduct wanting. She rebuked Prince Esterhazy for hogging the fire and not removing his hat, and despite the almost masculine vigour of her wit and energies, she preferred lovers whose manners were 'luxuriously sly and quiet'.

Too often we experience the past, especially the Regency period, through a veil of reverence. Not here. Harriette's story is told with gusto, more tabloid than tableau. It's totally compulsive reading, whether one is glimpsing celebs at the Drag Ball held to celebrate peace with Napoleon, hearing Harriette tell us that Wellington looked like 'a ratcatcher', or watching her fascinate whole regiments of officers. It's rather like eloping with Lydia Bennet instead of staying at home and, as Valerie Grosvenor Myer suggests, 'behind Becky Sharp lurks the ghost of Harriette Wilson's *Memoirs*, bowdlerised'.

But Harriette was a real person, not a literary creation, and her story could not have been more triumphantly unzipped, or more shamelessly and enjoyably displayed.

PREFACE

This is the real-life story of Harriette Wilson (1786–1845) the most famous courtesan of the Regency period, her heyday being 1800–1815. Professor John Bayley has chosen as his favourite opening words Harriette's: 'I shall not say why and how I became, at the age of fifteen, the mistress of the Earl of Craven', which begin her own sprightly *Memoirs*, on which this book is based. She was actually fourteen at the time. About dates she is frankly evasive, and they have had to be reconstructed or guessed at.

For example, Harriette says Lord Ebrington was a 'most enthusiastic admirer of Napoleon, to whom he said he had some idea of paying a visit on St Helena'. From other evidence within her account, this was in 1814, when Napoleon was on Elba, easily accessible from Italy, to which Ebrington was on his way. St Helena – the island to which Napoleon was banished after the battle of Waterloo in 1815 – is in the Atlantic, a thousand miles off the coast of Africa. Another source confirms that Lord Ebrington did visit Napoleon in 1814, and in 1823 published an account of their conversations on Elba. Harriette almost had it right. Her story is here interwoven with facts and anecdotes drawn from other memoirs, diaries and letters which throw light on Harriette or on her friends. I suggest (see Notes) that Harriette rearranged her narrative not only to show herself in a favourable light, but to hide the fact that several of her affairs occurred not in sequence but simultaneously. What else, she would have asked us, was a girl to do?

Harriette had enough style to be sought after as a mistress by noblemen who – although she rarely admits this – nevertheless treated her as disposable and usually married within their own class. However, she became the most celebrated serial mistress of her day. What was the secret of her fascination? After the publication of her *Memoirs*, the poet and novelist Sir Walter Scott described her as 'far from beautiful ... but a smart saucy girl with good eyes and dark hair, and the manners of a wild schoolboy'. Scott believed men sought her less for her looks than for her wit. He had met her twenty years previously, when she was in her prime, and concluded that her memoirs beat those of all former 'demi-reps in and out' – 'demi-reps' was a euphemism for women with no reputation left at all. Scott was amused that:

The gay [fashionable] world has been kept in hot water lately by the impudent publication of the celebrated Harriot [*sic*] Wilson, who lived with half the gay world at hack and manger, and now obliges such as will not pay hush-money with a history of whatever she knows or can invent about them (*Journal*, 9 December 1825)

If Jane Austen was the most celebrated 'good' girl of that day, Harriette was the most notorious naughty one. In a letter to her sister (Thursday 8 January 1801), sharp-eyed Jane noted that Lord Craven had a mistress living with him at Ashdown Park, Berkshire. This was Harriette Wilson, aged fourteen years and eleven months.

Socialite soldier Captain R H Gronow, in his famous *Reminiscences and Recollections*, which cover the first half of the nineteenth century, described her as 'a siren … one of the most notorious *traviatas* of the day', who 'had written her memoirs and become the scandal of the metropolis; one of her sisters had married a peer of the realm …' (Gronow, ed John Raymond, p 276).

Harriet, Countess Granville mentions in a letter (21 December 1820) 'a woman…of great beauty and celebrity, the Harriet [*sic*] Wilson of Vienna'. Lady Granville was the sister-in-law of the Duchess of Beaufort, whose son, the Marquis of Worcester, had been threatening to marry Harriette in 1812.

Much background information about Harriette comes from the *Confessions* of Julia Johnstone. Julia, a former friend of Harriette's, was horrified to read herself described as dead, with circumstantial detail, in Harriette's *Memoirs*, and rushed into print to dish the dirt. Julia admits to having been initially 'fascinated' by Harriette's 'lovely features and vivacity' (p 14), and says Harriette 'had the knack of pleasing' (p 115). Julia – whose portrait shows a pretty woman – was jealous of Harriette's notoriety and the fact that Harriette's book had made £10,000. Julia has had a bad press, because her attack is sanctimonious in tone and fuelled by jealousy. But despite her saying that Harriette lived with her family in Hammersmith when the records of ratepayers show them to have been in Mayfair, many of Julia's assertions make good sense. She shared a house with Harriette and knew her sisters – Amy, Fanny and Sophia – well. Every year the high-class trollops banded together and shamelessly threw the Cyprians' Ball at the Argyll Rooms in London. Julia's plight was to be a lady by birth and breeding, and a kept woman by necessity since, after being seduced at sixteen, she gave birth to eleven children, possibly by three different fathers.

Julia claims in her Introduction: 'I introduced her into fashionable life'; it was certainly Julia who introduced Harriette to Beau Brummell. Julia claims to have corrected Harriette's letters before they were sent and is responsible for the rumour that her publisher, Joseph Stockdale, known to be a rogue, wrote the 'brutish' parts of the Memoirs while Harriette wrote the 'licentious and gay'

'The celebrated Cyprians Ball was held every year at the Argyll Rooms. Here, Harriette's sister Amy is at the extreme right, and Harriette is standing up with the gentleman next to Amy

ones (*Confessions*, p 352). Julia does not say which is which. She sneers at Harriette's claims to be well-educated, and says she spoke French like a parrot with no knowledge of grammar. Julia's own French as printed is full of mistakes, but she quotes aptly from Pope and Shakespeare, which Harriette cannot do. However, Harriette left two novels, *Paris Lions and London Tigers* (1825) and *Clara Gazul* (1830), which show her to have been a fluent writer, though her plots are ramshackle. *Clara Gazul* – a title borrowed from Prosper Merimée – has a great deal of idiomatic and correct conversational French as then spoken by the English and Scottish upper classes – though, according to one commentator, ladies were careless about genders and endings. Many of Harriette's reported conversations in the *Memoirs* are in French and I have translated where necessary. Harriette's real flair was for dialogue, though her attempt to become a playwright was unsuccessful. Her own rollercoaster life story, selective and occasionally dishonest as her account of it is, supplied her with plenty of material.

Commentators have taken Harriette at her own valuation and sentimentalised her because she reproduces the speech of her contemporaries so vividly and is so shameless about her own approaches to likely prospects. At the same time she demanded formal rituals of 'introduction' and claimed 'respect'. The truth is she slept with lords for her living and, when she lost her looks, blackmailed them. She realized early that her chances of marriage to a man of 'polished refinement' were slim; gentlemen married girls with money, or at least those of birth and breeding.

Despite self-justifying hints that she was autonomous, an undertone of longing for love and a rich husband reverberates through the *Memoirs*, with a defiant pretence that she has no jealousy of those who achieved them. She says she is determined not to hurt Lady Ponsonby, her lover's wife, while – reading between the lines – we suspect that Harriette heartily wished her dead. She wants her beloved elder sister Fanny to be legally married, and is spiteful about her younger sister Sophia who, after being seduced by one peer at thirteen, married another at fifteen. Harriette is anxious to distinguish herself from 'common prostitutes' – from whom she seems to have differed only in being more expensive – and to emphasise her own fastidiousness. She claims to have been faithful to one man at a time, yet details specific infidelities as gestures of independence. She is to some extent 'in denial', as the saying goes.

Harriette's *Memoirs* caused a sensation, were eagerly read and violently attacked, and not only by Julia. A pamphlet of 1825, *Commentary on the Licentious Liberty of the Press in which the recent Publication entitled 'Memoirs of Harriette Wilson' is severely censured by a Student of the Inner Temple*, reads:

> A more disgusting and gross prostitution of the press cannot be … it may properly be called infamy exulting in its profligacy or pollution seeking a retribution for the hire of its vice … Is it not calculated to call forth the same offensive conduct in others?

Wicked Harriette may have been, especially when she became a blackmailer, but her entertaining *Memoirs* are tesserae in the mosaic of the Napoleonic era, with its gamblers, swindlers, dandies, eccentrics, pugilists, procurers, debauchees and aristocratic divorcees.

Cambridge 1999   Valerie Grosvenor Myer

1

LORD CRAVEN'S COCOA TREES

Lord Craven's fifteen-year-old mistress was bored and sulky. The year was 1801. She had made a bad bargain, escaping from a violent father and the drudgery of teaching music to live in a stately home with an 'elderly' man of thirty, of whom she was afraid. Having had two previous lovers – something she kept from Lord Craven – she knew what uncomplicated sexual pleasure could be – and she wasn't getting it. 'He's no fun,' she thought rebelliously, 'and that old cotton nightcap[1] of his makes him *ridiculous*!' She could not respond to his affection and, actually disliking his frigid and selfish embraces, preferred a good night's sleep.

Harriette was a jolie-laide, highly sexed and frank about it. Lacking social status, she had the natural advantages of a lovely figure, brown hair worn in stylish loose curls, dark-lashed hazel eyes and fashionably small hands and feet. Her slightly broad nose was tip-tilted, and she had a full and sensual mouth. She could be outrageously cheeky.

William Craven, seventh baron, was to become first earl the following year. A gallant and distinguished officer, Lord Craven had seen active military service in the West Indies as Lieutenant-Colonel of the 3rd Foot ('The Buffs') and only two years previously had been appointed aide-de-camp to King George III. Unfortunately, he drove his pretty girlfriend, half his age, nearly frantic as he droned on and on about his campaigns: 'Here stood the enemy, and here, my love, are my fellows. There are the cocoa trees ...' For young Harriette such wearisome lectures towards midnight were insufferable and she yawned uncontrollably. She fell asleep and muttered aloud: 'Oh Lord! Oh Lord! Craven has got me into the West Indies again.' Not that she had much to complain of apart from the boredom of hearing every day about fellows and cocoa trees, but neither her heart nor her senses was engaged, and she felt aggrieved.

Lord Craven liked to draw pictures of the battlegrounds on the best vellum paper, an extravagance which shocked Harriette. As one of fifteen children she had known poverty. It was early clear to her that pleasing men was a pleasanter way of making a living than mending stockings like her harrassed mother, Amelia, who had married at fourteen. Amelia was the illegitimate daughter of a gentleman, brought up by an aunt of the Duke of Argyll, Lady Frederick Campbell, who stood godmother to one of Harriette's sisters.

Harriot Dubochet or Dubouchet – who later reinvented herself, changing her surname to Wilson and Frenchifying her Christian name – was born in London on 22 February 1786 at 2 Carrington Street, Mayfair. Carrington Street no longer exists, but Mayfair is still one of London's most expensive districts, bordering Hyde Park, and home to some of Britain's grandest families. At the end of the eighteenth century Hampstead, Chelsea and Kensington were still villages among the surrounding fields. During Harriette's childhood the family moved to 23 Queen Street, Mayfair. Mrs Dubochet was having a hard time, as trousers gradually replaced knee-breeches and demand for stocking repairs declined. Even though the house was crowded with children, she took a lodger.

Harriette's father John Dubochet was a foul-tempered Swiss watchmaker who had left Switzerland after fighting a duel with an injured husband. Twenty years older than his wife, he met her when they lodged in the same house. Of noble descent, he resented his diminished status as a foreigner, and neglected his business to live off his browbeaten[2] wife and amuse himself with mathematics, despising his children for their lack of interest in the subject. Aged five, Harriet tore up a paper to make a fly-trap; the paper belonged to her father, who had written some calculations on it, which to him were precious. Characteristically egocentric, he thrashed her with a birch for this offence.

'Promise — not — to — do — it — again,' he panted between heavy blows.

'Say yes,' cried her poor crushed mother. 'Only say yes, child – it's easy enough to say yes, surely.'

'The devil must be got out of this child,' said her papa, holding her down and threatening her with the birch again.

'No!' she screamed at him, though she was bruised and bleeding. He dragged her upstairs, threw her on a bed and gave her another hiding. Then he pushed her away, grabbed her and locked her into a bedroom, but she would not be tamed.

'Let her out, please, John!' her mother pleaded. 'She's only a child. I'm sure she didn't realize how important that scrap of paper was.' Mrs Dubochet secretly agreed with her small daughter in thinking her husband's mathematical obsessions useless, but was anxious to keep the peace.

After several hours, the father grudgingly allowed the little girl out of her prison. She tells us: 'my body was disfigured from head to toe' and for two weeks she was 'stiff, feverish and full of pain'. In justice to Dubochet, savage corporal punishment for small children was customary at the time. He sulked, for the child had won the battle. Yet she loved him.

She did not love, nor even like, Lord Craven. He treated her like a possession and it never occurred to him to think about her feelings. He had been among her neighbours, living not far away in Mayfair, at 16 Charles Street[3], with his gambling brother, Berkeley Craven. Among Berkeley's friends was the popular man about town Tom Sheridan[4] son of the playwright. The Dubochet girls had known them – at least by sight – almost all their lives. Morning, noon and night, the older girls chattered about these handsome young men: 'How bright Berkeley Craven's eyes are!' 'What lovely soft hands Tom Sheridan has!' After undressing and cold-creaming her freckles, Harriette's red-headed elder sister Fanny would place herself in the old-fashioned ponderous armchair to read a love-letter from a cousin aloud, for the fiftieth time. At thirteen Harriette thought this repetitive conversation soppy, and mocked her sisters. They retaliated by jeering at her for being dark-skinned and straight-haired, even calling her 'ugly'.

Harriette took to sleeping in curl-papers, and began to take an interest in boys. Her first adventure was with the son of a washerwoman; he kept a small rowing-boat on the Thames below Hammersmith, where he plied for hire. Harriette's elder sister Amy used his boat for her regular visits to her own lover, an Isleworth miller famous for his virility. The girls travelled together on these journeys. Harriette was conscious of her father's 'blue blood' from his native Switzerland, and like him she looked down on the middle classes; later she prided herself on the elevated social status of her lovers. She confided to her friend Julia Johnstone that Lord Craven had been not her first lover, but her third. Startled, Julia – who herself had a genuine claim to gentility despite being an unmarried mother with five children – asked Harriette if this could be true. Harriette replied: 'True as eggs is eggs.' Harriette described the boy who had taken her virginity as a 'lusty, carroty lad' with fine strong teeth, adding: 'Then I fell sick for a recruiting sergeant who beat such a tattoo on my heart he fairly turned it topsy-turvy.' Harriette ran away with him, but he stole her clothes and her watch. 'This cooled her for low life, and she resolved to look higher,' says Julia sardonically.

Harriette's father, thinking she might be about to get into trouble, decided on a convent education for this defiant girl, and took her to Dieppe via Brighthelmstone[5], a three-day crossing in the days of sail. Adventurous Harriette wished she could go to India instead. On board she was seasick and confined to her cabin, while her father remained on deck. A handsome young aristocrat took care of her, until an old lady sent Mr Dubochet a warning that the young man's intentions might be less than honourable. John Dubochet began to play the heavy father and Harriette flared up at him, resenting this interference. She was beginning to understand that, however much her sisters might tease her about being 'ugly', she had sex appeal. At the convent she was popular with the nuns, but resisted all efforts to convert her to Roman Catholicism[6]. She was enchanted with the picturesqueness of France and the traditional costumes worn by peasant women.

When Harriette returned from abroad, she found her sister Amy had left home to live with a Mr Trench and another sister, Fanny, to live with a Mr Woodcock. The two respectable ones, Jane and Mary, nicknamed by Harriette

'Paragon and Diana', were still living with their parents, but they were, according to Harriette, 'peevish' because the household was hard up and its members quarrelsome. Harriette went to teach music at a girls' boarding school in Bayswater, but was soon tired of being 'nailed' to her chair from nine till three, listening to dull piano exercises out of tune and out of time. She left the place.

'I'm not having you eat the bread of idleness, my girl,' said her father. 'You must earn your own living.'

French she spoke and wrote fluently. Aged fourteen she went, escorted by Tom Sheridan, to teach French in a school at Newcastle upon Tyne run by a Miss Ketridge. Tom Sheridan was a soldier, travelling to join his General, Lord Moira[7], in Edinburgh.

'Please may I write to you?' begged Tom.

'If I wasn't being virtuous I wouldn't be going to Newcastle,' she replied. 'Plenty of London[8] gentlemen have offered to take me into keeping.' Then she softened.

'But I do want to get a love letter so badly.'

'Why?' asked Tom, amused.

'Because I want to pay my sister Fanny out. She read that love letter from our cousin out loud over and over till I was so sick of it that eventually I popped it into a meat pie on its way to the baker's.'

Tom laughed, but was touched, and promised her a letter which would be both affectionate and respectful.

Travelling by stage-coach was never comfortable, and this was winter. The journey took two days. On a freezing Saturday night the girl reached Ketridge House, a bleak and dismal place. After having gone through a wet kitchen, being scrubbed, she found the parlour, which had a very small fire. Miss Ketridge and the teacher of English, Miss Macdougal, were eating a frugal supper of Dutch cheese and small beer. Although she was hungry, Harriette did not fancy the meal, and chose to go instead to her bed. Miss Macdougal, a fat smiling woman in a Scottish plaid, showed Harriette to the room she was expected to share with another teacher.

'And you must be downstairs on the stroke of six for prayers, your bed already made.'

After a night spent shivering under inadequate blankets, Harriette broke the ice in the water jug and washed her hands and face, arriving as the clock struck six. After prayers which seemed interminable, she was disconcerted to see that breakfast consisted of one small roll.

'Is that all there is?' asked Harriette, astonished. 'I could do with another slice of bread.'

'Listen to the English miss!' mocked the other teachers, tittering. Next morning, trying to embarrass her, they put an eight-pound loaf on the table.

Cutting herself a generous slice, Harriette said nonchalantly, 'Brilliant, ladies, but it won't do. I'm not such a simpleton as to quarrel with my bread and butter.' This was hardly the way to recommend herself to her stingy employer, who ran a sweatshop; she required her staff to sew men's shirts during teaching periods and pocketed the money herself.

The building was miserably cold; the pupils illiterate. Harriette became ill. Miss Ketridge, who considered Harriette a troublemaker, sighed and, grumbling, called in an apothecary.

'This young lady needs to work shorter hours and drink milk still warm from the cow,' was his unwelcome advice.

'Too much sleep is unhealthy,' snapped Miss Ketridge. Harriette grew worse and eventually even her harsh father was sufficiently concerned by her agonized letters to let her go back to London. But she was nearly fifteen and needed a job.

She asked Tom Sheridan, now also returned to London, what she ought to do. He told her she looked like Sarah Siddons[9] and suggested she might go on the stage. He auditioned her himself, promising to use the influence of his famous father. Harriette borrowed a large waistcoat[10] from a coachman, stuffed it with a pillow, and read the part of Falstaff in Shakespeare's *Henry IV*, while Tom read Prince Hal, laughing till he cried. Mr Dubochet, however, stood on his precarious dignity.

'My daughter a rogue and a vagabond?' he roared. 'I'd rather see you dead in your grave!'

'Amy and Fanny are living comfortably in sin,' retorted Harriette. 'You expect me to carry on struggling to stuff children's heads with French irregular verbs?'

He threatened to thrash her for impertinence.

Attempting to please him, for he was her father after all, she decided she would cook him a specially delicious supper. But his comings and goings were unpredictable; that night he came home late in a bad temper and boxed her ears. This was the last straw. Harriette had had enough and decided at once to leave home, knowing her mother would understand. She had many admirers who were anxious to seduce her. She loved none of them, but among her old acquaintances were her neighbours, Lord Craven and his brother. In her own nonchalant words: 'They were gentlemen. I was less afraid of them than of any other men, so I became the mistress of Lord Craven.' With her adored mother's grim example before her, she was ambivalent about marriage.

When Craven moved to Marine Parade, Brighton, she went with him, but she was once more on the look-out for escape. Craven encamped with his regiment, for England was at war with France. His passion was sailing and his yacht *The Griffin* was a familiar sight from the Brighton shore. Brighton was fashionable, partly because the Prince of Wales spent so much time there. Lord

Craven also frequented the neighbouring village of Rottingdean. *The Sussex Weekly Advertiser* reported that Rottingdean in 1801 had been 'unusually full of company. The lovers of pure air, saline solution[11], and QUIET LIFE, will be sure of gratification.' A quiet life was everything the spirited Harriette did not want.

Vivacious Harriette attracted the attention of Craven's brother officers, aristocrats like himself, and began to look around her. The Honourable Frederick Lamb[12] was a constant visitor. Third son of Peniston, first Viscount Melbourne, he was educated at Eton and Trinity College, Cambridge, was knighted and eventually became third and last Viscount Melbourne. His elder brother William was Queen Victoria's first Prime Minister. Before succeeding to the title on William's death in 1848, Fred Lamb, clever and ambitious, pursued a distinguished diplomatic career in Bavaria, Madrid, Lisbon and Vienna.

The idea of deceiving Lord Craven with young Lamb while under Craven's roof was not seriously entertained by Harriette, although Frederick was both handsome and persistent. He tried to convince her that loyalty to Lord Craven was absurd. For the young bucks of the day, to cuckold a friend was part of the social game, and Fred was cynical by nature. Harriette was persuaded that he loved her and was sharp enough to regret that, as a younger son, he had no fortune to share with her. Harriette approved of Lord Melbourne, Fred's father, for not being strait-laced; he was not, she reflected gratefully, the moralising sort of father who would 'preach chastity and forbearance' to his children. On the contrary, he congratulated Fred on his luck.

'No such thing,' replied Frederick ruefully. 'I'm unsuccessful there. Harriette won't have anything at all to do with me.'

His father refused to believe it. 'Nonsense!' he growled. 'The girl must be mad. She looks mad. I thought so the other day when I saw her galloping about with her feathers blowing, and her hair about her ears … I'll speak to Harriette for you. Not have my son indeed! Six feet high! A fine, straight, handsome, noble young fellow!'

Harriette resented that Lord Craven had never said anything to please her nor once made her laugh. She was sick of his cocoa trees, sailing boats and cotton nightcaps. She wondered whether all men wore dreary nightcaps like his. If they did, every woman's illusions must surely be destroyed on the wedding night? Did the Prince of Wales wear a nightcap? Would he think her as beautiful as Fred Lamb did? She reflected that Fred, then still only twenty, was younger than the Prince, who was approaching forty … but then again, a Prince of Wales! Briefly she fantasised about going home, but knew her father would turn her out. Idly leafing through some papers, she found one covered with drawings of the detested cocoa trees. This exasperated her into writing to the Prince from Brighton:

I am told that I am very beautiful, so perhaps you would like to see me; and I wish that, since so many are disposed to love me, one, for in the humility of my heart I should be quite satisfied with one, would be at the pains to make me love him. In the meantime, this is all very dull work, Sir, and worse even than being at home with my father: so, if you pity me, and believe you could make me in love with you, write to me, and direct to the post office here.

The Prince's equerry replied:

Miss Wilson's letter has been received by the noble individual to whom it was addressed. If Miss Wilson will come to town, she may have an interview, by directing her letter as before.

Harriette's reply was impudent:

SIR, – To travel fifty-two miles in this bad weather, merely to see a man, with only the given number of legs, arms, fingers, &c, would, you must admit, be madness in a girl like myself, surrounded by humble admirers who are ever ready to travel any distance for the honour of kissing the tip of her little finger; but, if you can prove to me that you are one bit better than any man who may be ready to attend my bidding, I'll e'en start for London directly. So, if you can do anything better in the way of pleasing a lady than ordinary men, write directly: if not, adieu, Monsieur le Prince.

Harriette thought it more discreet to take this letter to the post herself, knowing that Lord Craven's black footman, Mungo, would be surprised to read the address. On her way to the post office, Harriette met Lord Melbourne who, after shaking hands with her, asked: 'Where is Craven?'

'Attending to his military duties at Lewes, my lord.'

'And where's my son Fred?'

'I'm not your son's keeper,' Harriette retorted.

'No? By the bye, what's going on? I never heard such a thing in my life! What have you got against Fred?' Lord Melbourne asked her. 'What the devil can you possibly have to say against him?'

'Good heavens, my lord, you frighten me! I can't remember saying a single word against your son. Why should I?'

'Why indeed!' cried Lord Melbourne. 'And since there's nothing to be said against him, what excuse have you got to offer for treating him so badly?'

Harriette was trembling; her experience of fathers had not been happy.

'I don't understand you in the least,' she stammered.

'Didn't you turn him out of the house as soon as it was dark? Craven was away, and you hadn't the shadow of an excuse — '

Harriette was astonished that a father's concern for his son's welfare could stretch so far. Before she could gather her wits, Fred joined them.

'Fred, my boy,' said Lord Melbourne, 'I'll leave you two together, and I fancy you'll find Miss Wilson more reasonable.' He touched his hat and went into the Brighton Pavilion.

Fred burst out laughing at his father's interference and so did Harriette, who told him she had refused the Prince of Wales, which amused Fred even more. He began to press his suit even harder.

'I must soon join my regiment in Yorkshire,' he said. He was aide-de-camp to General Mackenzie[13]. 'God knows when we'll meet again. I don't believe you'll stay with Lord Craven for long.'

Harriette was flattered, but still not attracted to Fred Lamb. Eventually, unable to put off his departure any longer, he asked permission to introduce his elder brother William[14] to Harriette.

'What for?' she asked.

'So he can keep an eye on you.'

'And if I fall in love with him?' asked Harriette archly.

Fred humourlessly replied that William was not likeable enough for that, although 'much handsomer than I am'.

Harriette spent more and more time with Fred, although she still resisted him. The result was that the footman soon brought a letter from Lord Craven at Lewes, when Harriette was expecting him back at any time. It read:

A friend of mine has informed me of what has been going on at Brighton. This information, added to what I have seen with my own eyes, of your intimacy with Frederick Lamb, obliges me to declare that we must separate. Let me add, Harriette, that you might have done anything with me with only a little more conduct. As it is, allow me to wish you happy; and further, pray inform me, if in any way, à la distance, I can promote your welfare.

CRAVEN[15]

Harriette was left in a situation both melancholy and embarrassing. Julia's spin on these events is different; she says that Craven threw Harriette out when he found her in bed with Mungo; and that the letter to the Prince of Wales was sent after she had left Craven for Fred. The equerry, Colonel Thomas, was a friend of Harriette's who later shot himself. Julia says Harriette coaxed Thomas into writing a 'reply' in order to make Fred jealous[16].

Notes to Chapter One

1. Page 7: Harriette took her revenge thirty years later; in her novel *Clara Gazul* the contemptible Italian marquis wears a nightcap – over his curl papers (vol 3, 214)! Referred to sometimes as a *roman à clef*, it is better described as a picaresque late-Gothic romance, a ragbag of castles, banditti, bastards and intrigue which owes much to *The Monk* (1796) by Matthew Lewis. Interspersed are lively and amusing sketches of London life, in which the Duke of Argyll – who owned Inverary Castle – appears as the Duke of Inverary, Lord Ponsonby as Lord Palatine, Lord Yarmouth as Lord Yellow-mouth, Lord Dudley as Lord Doolittle and Harriette's enemy the Duke of Beaufort as the Duke of Beaumont. Less easily recognized are Lords Ricketty and Pickle. There is even a self-portrait of 'Harriette Memoirs' in which she praises her own qualities as a 'high-spirited' woman whose voice was musical, who 'knew how to flatter' and was quick at repartee.

2. Page 8: The omniscient narrator of *Clara Gazul* says: 'All husbands consider their wives to be patient tools, destined to bear more harsh usage and insulting taunting remarks than the lowest menial would endure for an hour' (vol 1, 59).

3. Page 8: 16 Charles Street was later to become the Guards' Club.

4. Page 8: Tom Sheridan (1775–1817) was the only son of the celebrated playwright Richard Brinsley Sheridan (1751–1816), author of *The Rivals* and *The School for Scandal*. Tom was also a dramatist, author of *Bonduca*, produced at Covent Garden 3 May 1808. He was known as a practical joker. Samuel Rogers tells a story of his fixing a weathervane in the east in order to frighten a hypochondriac into staying indoors for a fortnight (*Table Talk*, p34). Tom married in 1805 Caroline Henrietta, daughter of Colonel James Callender, and died at the Cape of Good Hope when holding the post of Colonial Treasurer.

5. Page 9: pronounced as 'Brighton' after 1820, but earlier, according to Sylvester Douglas, first and last Baron Glenbervie of the Irish peerage, 'by all but vulgars, always called Brighthelmstone' (*Glenbervie Journals*, vol 2, 365). The Honourable Grantley F Berkeley preferred the 'old Brighton, with its limited accommodation, inconvenient houses, droll fashions, darkness and sedans' to its Victorian developments (*My Life and Recollections* , vol 1, 75).

6. Page 9: Harriette was staunchly Protestant, even if non-practising, and *Clara Gazul* carries characteristic nineteenth-century anti-Catholic baggage, including a licentious cardinal.

7. Page 10: Francis Rawdon-Hastings (1754–1826), first Marquis of Hastings and (in Irish peerage) second Earl of Moira. Soldier and Governor-general of Bengal, who in 1819 purchased the island of Singapore for Britain. Lord Glenbervie wrote of him:

Lord Moira has many qualities fit for … command. He is bold, and yet deliberate. He is very ambitious, and thirsts for both military and political fame. He has sufficient confidence in his own powers, and yet I do not believe he is obstinate or intractable. Though he has a lofty manner, which is a little beyond dignity, he affects popularity, and I have often observed that manners of that sort succeed better than the meretricious familiarity of some who, by too much courting of everybody, seldom gain anybody (*Journal*: 23 November 1793).

8. Page 10: Then pronounced 'Lunnon' (Samuel Rogers, *Table Talk*, p205).

9. Page 11: There may well have been some facial likeness to Mrs Siddons among the Dubochet girls, since Julia independently mentions Harriette's elder sister Amy as having a 'Siddonian countenance' (*Confessions*, p53). Sarah Siddons (1755-1831) was the most celebrated actress of her day.

10. Page 11: According to John Walker's *Pronouncing Dictionary* (1809 edn), 'waistcoat' was then pronounced 'weskot'.

11. Page 12: Sea-water was often drunk as a cure for various diseases.

12. Page 12: The Honourable Frederick James Lamb (1782–1853) was created Lord Beauvale in 1839. He married in 1848, when he was nearly sixty, Alexandrina, Countess von Maltzan, daughter of the Prussian Envoy to the Court of Vienna. To his social equals he could be charming, with polished courtesy. However, Harriet, Countess Granville wrote: 'I admire F Lamb perhaps more than I like him. I think him uncommonly agreeable and clever, but he sees life in the most degrading light, and he simplifies things by thinking all men rogues and all women [whores]' (letter to Lady Georgiana Morpeth, 28 August 1819). Nine years later she described him – by then Sir Frederick – as 'very ungracious and bitter and growling' (letter to the Duke of Devonshire, 13 December 1828). Fred's temper was not improved by gout; a decade later she noted that he had become 'as rude as a bear' (to her sister, Georgiana, who had become Countess of Carlisle, 14 September 1838).

13. Page 14: Fred Lamb was aide-de-camp to Major-General John Randoll Mackenzie (or McKenzie), who was killed at the battle of Talavera in 1809.

14. Page 14: William Lamb later married the eccentric Lady Caroline Ponsonby, famous for having responded to Byron's coldness by sending him snippings of her pubic hair in an envelope. A movie made about her in 1972 starring Sarah Miles omitted to mention this notorious packet, but showed her trying to attract Byron's attention by slashing her wrists in the Duke of Wellington's drawing room, a scene based on an incident which took place on 5 July 1813 when she tried to stab herself with a penknife at Lady Heathcote's ball. Lady Charlotte Bury wrote of her: 'When she is free of these [melancholy] attacks, nobody can be more agreeable, and her conversation is both original and superior' (*Memoirs of the Times of George IV*, 16 January 1820). Elizabeth,

Lady Holland, the great Whig hostess, was more severe: 'She was not mad, only wicked from temper and brandy' (cited in Sonia Keppel's biography, *The Sovereign Lady*, p259).

15. Page 14: Lord Craven married Louisa Brunton, an actress, in December 1807. Her father was originally a greengrocer in Drury Lane, but later became manager of the Norwich Theatre, where Louisa appeared with great success.

16. Page 14: *Confessions*, p28. Julia also says Harriette frequently wrote flattering letters to herself.

2

The Honourable Fred Lamb and the Marquis of Lorne

Harriette replied to Craven's letter at once:

> … In the plenitude of your condescension, you are pleased to add that I 'might have done anything with you, with only a little more conduct' … the Lord defend me from ever doing anything with you again! Adieu,
>
> HARRIETTE

She was glad to be rid of the cocoa trees, and told herself she hated cocoa, Craven's carriage and even his money. She vowed never to get on a boat again if she could help it.

'This is what one gets by acting with principle,' she told herself. Meanwhile, she was homeless and penniless. Rescue soon arrived via a letter from Fred Lamb in Hull. She set out at once. Fred welcomed her warmly and she lived under his protection in Hull, where his regiment was stationed. According to Julia, Harriette made a nuisance of herself, frequenting the parade ground and flirting with the officers. After three months Fred and Harriette returned to London, where he established her in lodgings with an old widow at Duke's Row, Somers Town, near the present St Pancras railway station, an area then surrounded by fields. In the evenings he left her to pine alone while he frequented dinners, balls and masquerades. She longed for love and for an entrée into fashionable society. Men moved easily between two worlds, but girls like Harriette could hardly enter respectable circles. Fred hid his mistress away in this unfashionable quarter, inhabited mainly by French refugees, and kept her short of money[1]. Soon the widow had given Harriette all the leeway on the rent she could.

Aristocratic society at the time consisted of close intermarried networks. The people whom Fred knew and whom Harriette was to know later all knew each other and passed mistresses from hand to hand. Sulky once more, she asked him: 'Is the Marquis of Lorne[2] as handsome as everybody says?'

'All the women adore him,' said Fred, who was planning to go out of London for several weeks, leaving Harriette in extreme poverty. In a fit of pique, Harriette wrote to Lorne saying that if he would walk to Duke's Row,

The handsome Marquis of Lorne, later sixth Duke of Argyll

Somers Town, he would meet a 'most lovely girl'.

He replied inviting her to call on him at 39 Portland Street. She wrote back that she preferred the road, so that if necessary she could run away. He suggested meeting her on horseback, so he could gallop away. They met and she was enchanted by his manly beauty – for he had classically elegant features – and by the polished refinement she hankered for in men. They walked together for a couple of hours.

'May I call on you at home?' he asked.

'And how will your great friend Fred Lamb like that?' she retorted.

Lorne laughed and invited her to dinner at his house.

'I shan't be able to run away if I go there!' laughed Harriette.

'Shall you want to run away from me?' said Lorne tenderly, with an intense look that made Harriette blush. He told her how lovely her happy face was and enjoyed seeing her blush again, attracted by her boldness. They agreed to know each other better, and to meet again next day. Harriette was elated. Then her conscience told her she had wronged her protector. It struck her it was too late – she was seventeen – to become a steady, prudent, virtuous woman. She decided that she was 'unfortunate'[3] already, but resolved to be unlike other fallen women in staying honest and in loving truth. I will never become vile, she thought, and when I am ill-treated I will leave my lover rather than deceive him; I must tell Fred about Lorne when he comes home tonight.

Fred, far from being angry, was flattered at the idea of possessing a woman he assumed Lorne would sigh for in vain. He called Harriette 'my dearest little wife', and said: 'I know I can trust you as safely with him as Craven could trust you with me. You must punish him for saying that he is only interested in women who fall for him on sight!'

'I'm sorry he's so conceited!'

'What's that to you, you little fool?'

Harriette reflected that Lorne's silky manner and dark blue eyes already haunted her fancy and her dreams.

'Your figure's better than his,' she said slily.

'He's getting fat,' said Fred smugly, 'although he takes plenty of exercise.'

'So you don't mind my walking with him? You're not jealous?'

'I want to have a laugh at his expense; I'm sure of your affections.'

Harriette found this depressing; her only excuse for leaving Fred would be if he should leave her totally destitute, but her feelings drew her to Lorne. Lorne angered her, however, by not turning up next day. She wrote complaining, and he replied that an accident had held him up, but making another date. She kissed the letter and put it in her bosom. Fred had praised her firm white breasts with their small pink nipples and held them in his hand; what would Lorne say when he was allowed to see and caress them? She tingled at the thought. She had had relations with four men, yet was experiencing new emotions. Could this be love? She stood Lorne up next time to teach him a lesson, nonetheless, and told Fred what had happened. Fred, expecting to meet Lorne at Lady Holland's dinner party that evening, planned to mock his humiliation.

Next morning Harriette heard not from Lorne but from Tom Sheridan. Fred had left for his father's country house, Brocket Hall in Hertfordshire, so Harriette invited Tom to call. Tom carried Lorne's apology; at the last minute the Prince of Wales had invited him to his London residence, Carlton House, and Lorne did not want to write to Harriette for fear she might show the letters to Fred.

'You'll make it up with Lorne, won't you?' said Tom. 'What a pretty girl you are, especially when you blush! I believe he's in love with you.' Tom told Harriette that he, Tom, was consumptive and off to the warm Mediterranean. 'I'm dying,' he said. She begged him to drink less heavily.

Tom mocked her: 'Did you see me play the Methodist parson at Mrs

Beaumont's masquerade last Thursday?'

'You can laugh at me if you like, but I admire you and I'm sorry to see your time misspent and your brilliant talents misapplied,' persisted Harriette, who was fond of him.

'What a funny little girl you are! Pray, miss, how is your time spent?'

'Not in drinking brandy,' said Harriette.

'My good little girl, it's in the blood and I can't help it, and if I could it's too late now. I'm dying, I tell you. I don't know if my poor father's physician is as eloquent as you are, but he did his best to turn him from drinking. He declared that the brandy he swallowed would burn off the coat of his stomach. My father said: "Then my stomach must digest in its waistcoat". '

She leaned her face towards him. He parted her thick, dark hair and kissed her forehead, her eyes and her lips.

'If I do come back,' he said, forcing a smile, 'mind you let me find you married, and rich enough to lend me an occasional hundred pounds – or even two.' He kissed his hand gracefully and was out of sight in an instant.

Despite Tom's complaint, he married in 1805, fathered four sons and three daughters, and lived till 1817. But Harriette never saw him again.

Next morning Harriette's maid brought a note from Lorne, who was waiting in the street. She looked out of the window, ran for her hat and cloak, and met him at once.

'Am I forgiven?' he asked tenderly.

'Oh yes, but it won't do you any good. I can't go on walking with you; I'm treating Fred very badly.'

'You told Fred I walked about looking for you, just to make him laugh at me!'

'No, it's not that. I'm not deceitful; it's me who thinks it wrong to be with you, not Fred.' Her heart was thumping.

'You think me a bore,' said Lorne, reddening.

'Fred trusts me.'

'If you loved me, you'd forget him easily enough. You must promise to try and fall in love with me some day; I've set my heart on that, you know.'

These romantic walks continued for a month. One evening they stayed out after dark, and Lorne caught her in his arms. Long-desired, his hungry kisses set her aflame. He ventured further and she could barely contain herself. But when he attempted to grope her skirt, she took offence.

'You don't respect me!' she cried.

A perfect gentleman, Lorne desisted.

'Oh I do, I do,' he groaned, kissing her hair, her ears, her eyes, clutching her tightly round the waist. 'It's just that I find you irresistible. You little witch! You've cast a spell on me, I do believe.'

Harriette breathed deeply. His wandering hands had stirred and thrilled her as neither Craven's nor Fred's had done. Her private parts were accessible, for few ladies in her generation wore drawers[4]. Her stockings were gartered at the knee, and her bare thigh tensed with response at his touch, even through her petticoat. The pleasure of Lorne's tentative and unfulfilled caress was more exquisite and satisfying even than the simple rutting she had enjoyed with the carroty lad and the recruiting sergeant. For the moment, power was hers, and she had no intention of being too easily won. The moment was delicious and she wanted to prolong it, though her senses longed for full satisfaction. She felt the pressure of his erection hard against her own soft belly and smiled to herself. Blood sang in her ears; her nipples rose unbidden in response; her clitoris swelled, throbbed and ached. She squeezed her own thighs tightly together and enjoyed the sensation. Not yet awhile, my lord, she said to herself, although she was wet for him. She imagined the joy of yielding, when she would melt into Lorne's arms. Meanwhile, she scolded him for insulting her. He grovelled. Harriette went home pleased with herself, leaving him to think she was in a huff.

Lorne knew how to tease her in return. Next morning's note from him read:

If you see me waiting about your door tomorrow morning, do not fancy
I am looking for you, but for your pretty housemaid.

Harriette watched from a sly corner of her window. In the cold light of day she decided she must resist her own aching desire – Fred might kill her! She wrote to Lorne saying she had never loved anybody before, sending a lock of hair, and suggesting they must part, since mere friendship between them was impossible. Lorne replied that he was the 'last man on earth to desire you to do violence to your feelings by leaving a man as dear to you as Frederick Lamb is, so farewell Harriette … '

Lorne was teased by his smart friends about Harriette and a crowd of them rode into the area while Lorne was sitting on a gate near her door, whistling. He was hoping to meet her as it were by accident. They mocked him until they were interrupted by an old mad Frenchman, who had often seen him walking with Harriette, and who now screamed at him as 'Monsieur le Comte Dromedaire' (Campbell being then pronounced 'camel') and asked where was 'Madame la Comtesse'. Lorne diverted his anger on to this poor old man, who ran away on 'spider-legs'. Fred was angry with Harriette for not finding this story amusing, but Harriette was grateful to Lorne for having put up with ridicule for her sake.

Fred was more obsessed with her than ever. He sometimes read to her in the evenings (Milton, Shakespeare, Byron, Dr Johnson and Vergil) and Harriette played the pianoforte to him. She was untaught, but quick-witted and musical, and able to play by ear. She says she was out walking one day when she met

Julia Johnstone, who had overheard her playing and complimented her on it[5]. Julia was about twenty-five, always expensively and tastefully dressed, elegant but isolated, living not far away in a charming cottage, with five beautiful children who walked out with their nurse, dressed to the nines.

Julia Storer, 'Mrs Johnstone', author of 'Confessions'
which gives another slant on Harriette's reminiscences

'You are the first female I have spoken to for four years with the exception of my own servants,' said Julia. Her voice was cultivated and sweet. She invited Harriette to dinner. Harriette was struck with the fine taste of Julia's home furnishings; there was a fine pianoforte, a beautiful harp, embroideries, drawings 'of a somewhat voluptuous cast' – Harriette's own words – and a volume of Tom Moore's poems. She's not a 'bad woman', thought Harriette to herself, but she's not a 'good woman', either. What and who could Julia be?

They were sitting down to dinner when 'Mr Johnstone' arrived, a handsome man in middle age. His manner towards Julia seemed to Harriette that of a romantic lover rather than a husband. Julia was altogether a mystery. Harriette asked her why she had invited a stranger to dinner.

'Consider the melancholy life I lead,' said Julia. 'Shall we go to the nursery?' Harriette romped with the five children, dressing their dolls and teaching them to skip. She forgot about Lorne as she developed this new friendship.

Julia, despite her shyness, called on Harriette next day. Every inch a lady, Julia had a fair, delicate skin, pretty arms, small hands and feet – much prized in those days – and a graceful figure. She struck the observant Harriette as a woman of violent passions, despite her reserve and retirement. 'Mr Johnstone' came about twice a week, walking across the fields while Julia and Harriette – who was still left much alone by Fred – waited on a gate to welcome him. The meetings between Julia and her lover were full of 'rapturous and romantic delight', says Harriette. Soon the two women met every day and exchanged life stories.

Julia's real name was Storer. She was the daughter of the Honourable Mrs Storer, sister to Lord Carysfort. Mrs Storer had been Lady-in-Waiting to Queen Charlotte, wife of King George III. Julia was educated in France, and at sixteen had been sent to the Palace of Hampton Court by her mother on a visit to the wife of Colonel Cotton, an officer in the 10th Dragoons, a very smart regiment, later the Prince of Wales's Own. Mrs Cotton was the mother of nine children and did not want any more; she was finding it hard to make ends meet. Julia fell madly in love with the sex-starved Colonel Cotton, who pounced. In four months she was pregnant, but managed to hide her pregnancy for the full term. She was paying her respects to Queen Charlotte when her waters broke, causing a sensation. Mrs Cotton screamed abuse at her.

'Please send for a midwife!' pleaded Julia.

'I'll do no such thing,' declared Mrs Cotton. 'Think of the disgrace to your family. You deceitful little whore, coming into a respectable household, making yourself cheap to a decent man! You made your own bed, my girl, or rather climbed into mine, and now you can lie on it.'

Julia somehow got to her own room. Mrs Cotton slammed the door. Julia, still only sixteen, was left alone during her five-hour labour and delivered her son herself. Her noble relatives were outraged, Julia was hustled away to the country, and her brother challenged Colonel Cotton to a duel, in which the Colonel was wounded, though not badly. Julia managed to write to her lover, threatening to kill herself if he abandoned her. After nine years and five children, they were still romantically in love. He wrote her passionate letters, which she showed to Harriette, who laughed at them. Julia lived on the interest of her own inherited £4,000.

When Harriette was down on her luck, she slept at Julia's house. Julia gives us a glimpse of Harriette preparing for bed:

> She was a perfect nightmare in the same room with you, taking as much pains in doing up her fine hair and folding her laced nightgown and cap as though she were preparing for a ballroom. I remonstrated with her once on the folly of spending two hours thus, and then waking me up out of my sleep to give my opinion on how her nightclothes became her, whether she looked most like Cleopatra waiting for Antony, or the wife of Potiphar trying to seduce Joseph. Harriette said she would not for the world go to bed otherwise than elegant, for fear of dying in the night and not making an elegant corpse[6].

Meanwhile Lorne was teased by the men about town and was feeling angry at Harriette's rejection of him. He was bored and vexed about the time he had lost, yet kept returning to Harriette's neighbourhood, hoping to meet her once again by accident and then give her up. Harriette's finances were sinking low; she had sold all the trinkets Craven had given her. She wrote to Lorne inviting herself to dinner on a day she knew Fred would be visiting his father. Lorne accepted at once and met her at their old rendezvous, the turnpike.

His reception of her was very different from that of Fred Lamb in Hull. Fred had been all wild passion; Lorne was gentle, timid, soft-spoken, fearful of shocking her or of frightening away her growing desire for him. She floated on dreams of ecstasy. He promised in French to send his carriage for her in future. He was not a rich man till he inherited the dukedom of Argyll in 1806; his clothes were frayed and threadbare, and he had an old horse, an old groom, an old carriage and an old house in Argyll Street. But he was good-looking, well-bred and charming. After dinner they went to bed and at last Lorne saw Harriette naked.

'Delectable creature,' he breathed delightedly. She was even more beautiful than he had imagined. He kissed her all over, lingeringly. He was enchanted by her firm young breasts, and small pink nipples like rosebuds.

'I'm not a disappointment to you, then?' she asked coquettishly, surveying herself in the mirror, wearing only her lover's hat.

'You were worth the wait,' he said, respectfully kissing her pretty hand with its almond nails and pronounced mount of Venus. Unlike Craven, Lorne knew how to give pleasure as well as take it. Fred Lamb went at it like a bull at a gate, but Lorne knew how to take his time. His sensitive hands strayed wherever they fancied – above, between, below, this time without rebuke – and brought her to orgasm even before she guided him into what the eighteenth-century sex manual, *Aristotle's Masterpiece*, called 'love's dark channel'[7]. She gave a loud cry. They made love several times, each time better than the last, and slept late.

Harriette was pleasurably sore for days.

Pleased with Lorne, passion satisfied, and proud of her conquest, Harriette went home and told Fred Lamb. Fred was so self-centred he believed Harriette to be in love with him, whereas he had been to her merely a port in a storm.

'You said he was irresistible,' said Harriette perkily.

'Yes, yes, yes,' muttered Fred between gritted teeth, 'but a woman who loves a man is blind to every other. Still, I'm glad it has happened –'

'Did I ever say I was in love with you? It was not I who deceived you, but your vanity. You were responsible for my losing Lord Craven's protection, so I came to you. I've never loved you nor any man before this. I might have felt a sisterly affection for you, but you never bothered to ask whether or not I was happy. I won't be a mere instrument of pleasure for any man. My lover must treat me as a friend and companion, or he'll lose me.'

Fred's refusal or – as she saw it – neglect to take her to smart parties rankled. No respectable matron could have received her, she being a kept woman on the disreputable fringes of society. Having drifted into her role, she did not yet grasp its implications. Harriette screamed at him: 'You drink champagne and don't care whether I've got bread and cheese!' Fred parted from her in a rage. After the first part of her *Memoirs* was published, Fred called on Harriette's publisher 'to threaten him, or us, with prosecution, death and destruction' – in Harriette's own words – if his name was allowed to appear again. Fortunately for posterity, he could not afford to sue.

Fred, discussing Harriette with Julia, said: ''Tis a pity so beautiful a casket should hold nothing within it, no gem worth picking the lock for … she has no heart for anything but flattery and fine clothes … I once loved her and wished to love her; but… he who keeps her must keep her for show … a puppet[8]'. 'She threw off lovers as indifferently as she changed her shoes[9]', adds Julia: Harriette 'threw away guineas as I would pence'; she 'borrowed £300 from old Courtois, the hairdresser … a rank old debauchee' from whom she had jewels to the value of £800. He claimed £300 from Fred, who paid up. Courtois threatened to arrest Harriette for the sum outstanding, but after she had disappeared with him for an hour above the shop, was 'all smiles', kissing her hand and calling her 'very kind, very pretty[10]'.

Harriette took a furnished house in the west end of London to receive Lorne, who was besotted with her, but not quite besotted enough to give up his titled mistress of many years standing. He wrote to tell Harriette that he could not 'be entirely yours', which provoked her into thinking perhaps she would not be entirely his. Julia says Fred abandoned Harriette leaving her desperate for money, adding that Lorne gave Harriette £50 and a diamond ring, which made her hope for marriage, but he was too poor to be depended on. Lorne sat with this other woman – whom we know only as 'Lady W—', in her box at the opera, wearing a chain Lady W— had given him. Harriette's jealousy made her steal this chain and hide it. She could not bear the idea that all the tenderness and passion Lorne seemed to feel for her was shared with the other woman. One night at Argyll House in bed with Lorne she threatened to go home.

'You must be sleepwalking!' said Lorne, putting on his dressing gown and preparing to restrain her.

'I'm not asleep,' said Harriette, bursting into tears, 'I can't stay here. I'd rather die.'

'What have I done to offend you?'

'Nothing; just leave me alone. I can't bear this show of tenderness.'

'Gracious God, how you torment me! Do I disgust you? Have you stopped loving me?' said Lorne, distressed.

Harriette said nothing.

He implored her to speak. His agitation astonished her. This man, she thought, is either very nervous or he loves me just as I want to be loved. Her hand was on the door knob. Lorne crossed the room, took hold of her and flung her on to the bed. Locking the door, he snatched the key and pocketed it.

'By heavens,' he said, 'you shan't torture me another moment!'

Moving back to the bed, he pressed her roughly to him, leaving bruises on her arms. She thought he was going to kill her and looked up at him like a frightened animal. He pushed her gently away and burst into tears himself. Smiling through his tears, he captivated Harriette once more.

'I'm not tired of you, dear Lorne!' she cried. 'How could I be? Forgive me, forgive me …

Their reconciliation was completed, writes Harriette demurely, 'in the usual way.'

Notes to Chapter Two

1. Page 18: Julia says Fred allowed Harriette £100 a month and paid all her dressmakers' and millinery bills at Christmas (*Confessions*, p31). Julia insists there 'is nothing more ridiculous than the efforts Harriette makes to convince the world that her amours were carried on for love and that she despised money' (p327). According to Julia, when Harriette was tracked down by a creditor, Sir Thomas Lavie, she snatched her IOU from his hand and swallowed it (p318).

2. Page 18: George William Campbell, Marquis of Lorne (1776–1839), was ten years older than Harriette, and at that time far from well off. On 10 May 1804 his father wrote him a reproachful letter after paying Lorne's debts.

> … In return I expect your solemn promise and declaration that you will never again play for any higher sum than twenty pounds in one day … The principal cause of your misfortunes is the habit … of keeping very bad hours. They tend to drunkenness, and that to Gambling and every ruinous folly. The best remedy is marriage, which if you can find a woman to your mind would keep you at home. I most earnestly recommend it to you. I will share everything with you for the short time I have to linger here. Adieu. Most affectionately yours,
>
> ARGYLL

Elizabeth Lady Holland's *Journal* (13 January 1800) says: 'Lord Lorne is an old favourite of mine; his good humour, cheerfulness and ease is quite charming. ['Monk'] Lewis's lines in an epilogue to *Barbarossa*, which they acted at Inverary, are very descriptive of him:

> And Lord Lorne's easy air, when he got in a passion,
> Proved a tyrant must needs be a person of fashion.'

Lorne succeeded his father to become sixth Duke of Argyll in 1806, inheriting vast estates in Scotland. Gronow lists him among the dandies along with Lord Alvanley and the Marquis of Worcester, a later lover of Harriette. Despite appearing fashionably insouciant, Lorne raised a militia in 1792, and became Vice-Admiral of the West Coast of Scotland and Keeper of the Great Seal.

When he died in 1853, the diarist Greville wrote of him:

> Very handsome in youth, clever, agreeable and adroit, he was much addicted to gallantry and had endless liaisons with women, most of whom continued to be his friends long after they had ceased to be his mistresses … He was largely endowed with social merits and virtues, without having or affecting any claim to those of a higher or moral character.

Charles Cavendish Fulke Greville (1794–1865) is the most famous of the Regency diarists. Educated at Eton and Christ Church, Oxford, he was a page to King George III. He was a revealing and eloquent but censorious commentator.

3. Page 20: An 'unfortunate' was a nineteenth-century euphemism for a prostitute. Thomas Hood's poem *The Bridge of Sighs*, about a homeless streetwalker who has drowned herself in the Thames, begins:

> One more Unfortunate
> Weary of breath
> Rashly importunate,
> Gone to her death!

A young woman asked her occupation by the Victorian sociologist Henry Mayhew replied: 'I'm unfortunate, sir.'

4. Page 22: Women did not generally wear knickers till mid-century, and not always then. 'Walter', in *My Secret Life* (vol 13), laments that servant girls have begun to wear them, depriving him of 'chance feels of bum and cunt'.

5. Page 23: Julia's account of her meeting with Harriette is more likely to be true; she says Tom Sheridan introduced Colonel Cotton – 'Mr Johnstone' – to Harriette, and Cotton took Harriette to meet Julia at the cottage at Primrose Hill where she lived in seclusion: 'We were as friendly as two sisters, and every evening when Frederick Lamb left her alone, which was four out of six, she came to me, danced to my music and romped with the children' (*Confessions*, p20).

6. Page 25: *Confessions*, p227.

7. Page 25: *Aristotle's Masterpiece*:

> My rudder with thy bold hand, like a try'd
> And skilful pilot, thou shalt steer and guide,
> My bark in love's dark channel, where it shall
> Dance, as the bounding waves do rise and fall.

8. Page 26: *Confessions*, p227.

9. Page 26: *Confessions*, p36.

10. Page 26: *Confessions*, p45.

3

THE THREE GRACES

Julia was soon introduced to Harriette's favourite sister, Fanny. Lord Yarmouth, later Marquis of Hertford, always insisted she was the best-looking of that handsome family: 'That laughing dark blue eye of hers is uncommonly beautiful,' he was fond of saying. Harriette loved Fanny, four years older than herself, deeply. An unintegrated biographical scrap turns up in the novel *Clara Gazul*: 'She is dead now, poor pretty Fanny: – her blue laughing eyes are closed – her Swiss father was too severe[1]'.

Julia despised Fanny as a:

> poor, timid, good-natured thing, incapable of doing either harm or good. She scarcely knew the distinction between virtue and vice; whenever she did good, it was from accident; when she committed evil, it was from want of knowing better, and she had a vacant see-saw way of thinking that everything happened for the best. If you could not love her, it was impossible to hate her[2].

A Mr Woodcock had fallen for Fanny's blue eyes and ginger curls and wanted to marry her. He was, though, married already, in a day when the divorce laws were inelastic: divorce was available only to the rich and powerful[3]. He and Fanny had three children, but after seven years Woodcock died.

Julia, Fanny and Harriette were soon seen about together and took their own box at the opera at a seasonal fee of £200 at a time when a labourer's weekly wage, on which he had to maintain his wife and family, was ten shillings (50p). An opera box was a showcase for aristocracy and demi-mondaines alike. They were nicknamed the Three Graces, and might have been a foursome if the eldest sister, Amy, had been friendlier.

Raven-haired, statuesque Amy had first taken up with a Mr Trench, whom she met in the street after running away from her grim father. When Harriette and Fanny discovered where Amy was living, they asked her what had induced her to throw herself away on a stranger. She replied: 'I refused him the whole of the first day; if I'd done so the second, he'd have got a fever.' Mr Trench tried without success to train her to be economical, so she eloped with General Madden, claiming to be faithful to him over several years. One evening when the General was away Harriette found a pair of breeches at Amy's labelled

Raven haired Amy, Harriette's elder sister

'Proby'. When Harriette asked what Lord Proby's 'small-clothes' were doing there, Amy threw her out[4]. 'Amy's virtue was something like the nine lives of a cat,' writes Harriette. Julia is blunter, calling her 'a modern Messalina[5]' and a 'masculine spirit, proud and avaricious'. Madden, who at the time was abroad, could not stand Harriette, because she was 'always at her window like the sign of Queen Elizabeth over a tavern door, to invite passers-by to walk in'. Although Madden was poor, Amy often had three hundred or more pounds in her pocket. The Russian diplomat Count Benckendorff wanted to 'marry her with the left hand' – that is, take her as his mistress.

'Why not with the right?' asked Amy

'I daren't,' he told her solemnly, 'without the consent of the Emperor of Russia.'

Believing this excuse, Amy urged him to go back to his country to get permission. Julia knew that Russian nobles could marry whom they liked, and laughed in her sleeve. Amy gave parties to fashionable men after the opera. Parsimonious Amy was forced, according to Harriette, to invite her sisters in order to brighten her parties with their grand men-friends. Harriette sneers at Amy and her parties, but nevertheless Amy managed to run some sort of salon and Harriette, who did not entertain, took advantage of it.

Lord Nugent, 'Fat Nugent', at Oxford University

'Fat' Nugent[6], with his everlasting laugh, wished Amy would dismiss some of her 'dirty Russians' – who included Count Woronzow[7] and the Russian ambassador, Count Orloff. Nugent was younger son of the first Marquis of Buckingham, who succeeded to his mother's Irish peerage in 1813. He was always accompanied by the writer and epigrammatist Colonel Henry Luttrell[8], an illegitimate son of the second Earl of Carhampton, and valued for his brilliant conversation, often peppered with outrageous puns. He was described by Gronow as 'the most agreeable man I ever met … He was extremely irritable and even passionate; and in his moments of anger he would splutter and stutter like a maniac in his anxiety to give utterance to the flow of thoughts which crowded his mind, and, I might almost say, his mouth'[9]. This does not sound attractive, but he was a writer and friend of Byron and the poet Thomas Moore. His cynical façade concealed a kind heart, and he was considered ugly but delightful.

One night at the opera Lord Alvanley[10], the celebrated dandy and wit, introduced a tall, well-dressed foreign gentleman to Harriette merely as his 'friend'.

'That won't do, Lord Alvanley,' said Harriette. 'That is no introduction, and less recommendation. Name your friend, or away with him.'

'Really, madam,' replied the stranger in French, 'a name is not important. I stand before you, an upright man of five feet nine inches.'

'The lady knows about your five feet, but she's not sure of your nine inches,' quipped Alvanley, also in French. Selfish and snobbish, but urbane, he had a snub nose and spoke with a lisp. The diarist Thomas Creevey[11] called him 'a natural wag'; the diarist Greville wrote of him that he was 'reckless and profligate about money; he cared not what debts he incurred'. Alvanley, like George Brummell, eventually found himself so in debt that he was forced to live in France and suffered the humiliation of being blackballed by a Paris club. He insisted on having cold apricot tart served every day of the year.

On one occasion, finding the 'Three Graces' eating their dinner at six, Alvanley said: 'Who the devil dines at six? I'm only just out of bed!' He was a typical Regency buck, who fought a duel with the son of a man who called him 'a bloated buffoon'. On the way back, he gave the hackney coachman a sovereign. The man protested it was too much. 'It is not for taking me there, my good fellow, but for bringing me back,' said Alvanley[12]. Anecdotes of Alvanley's witticisms are scattered through the memoirs of the period: most of them travel as badly across the years as that one.

He was notorious for reading in bed by candlelight and throwing the candle down or putting it, still alight, under the bolster. When he stayed in country houses, servants had to stay awake all night outside his room, in case of fire. He was, says Gronow, 'the idol of the clubs', but not presumably of the servants, though his equals agreed in finding him charming.

While various lordly men were flirting with Harriette, who was smiling brilliantly and pretending not to see Lorne in his box with the detested Lady W—. Julia received no attention. She was largely ignored because she was shy, short-sighted and the eldest of the three. Eventually Julia kissed her hand to somebody.

'Who are you bowing to?' asked Harriette.

'An old flame of mine, who was violently in love with me when I was a girl at Hampton Court,' whispered Julia. 'I've never seen him since I've known Cotton.'

'What's his name?'

'George Brummell,' answered Julia. Harriette had never heard of him. He joined them and showed delight on seeing Julia although, as Harriette observed later, he was indifferent to women. 'Beau' Brummell was a skilled and ruthless social climber, who bullied the Prince Regent and dominated London society. Himself of slender means, he set a style of elegance slavishly followed by his social superiors. Harriette describes him as 'extremely fair', but not good-looking because of his broken nose. She quotes him as saying:

'No perfumes, but very fine linen, plenty of it, and country washing.'

'If John Bull turns round to look after you, you are not well dressed: but either too stiff, too tight, or too fashionable.'

She leaves us this shrewd sketch:

> … his maxims on dress were excellent … He possessed … a quaint, dry humour, not amounting to anything like wit; indeed, he said nothing which would bear repetition; but his affected manners and little absurdities amused for the moment. Then it became the fashion to court Brummell's society, which was enough to make many seek it who cared not for it; and many more wished to be well with him through fear, for all knew him to be cold, heartless and satirical.

Brummell was one of a group that included Lord Alvanley, Lord Craven, the Marquis of Worcester (later Duke of Beaufort) and Lord Yarmouth (later Marquis of Hertford) who were favourite weekend guests at Oatlands, the country house of the Duke and Duchess of York[13]. In his pose of treating trivial matters as serious and serious matters as trivial, Brummell paved the way towards decadence, yet he set the pattern of quiet good taste and dark colours in men's clothing which lasted until the outbreak of flower-power and hippie gear in the 1960s and 70s. He was creative only in lifestyle, which in the end failed him when he was banished, like Falstaff, from the royal presence.

That there should be so many competing versions of Brummell's insolent remarks, and of the circumstances surrounding the famous insult 'Who's your fat friend?' directed at the Prince, is evidence that Brummell was a legend in his own lifetime. Other men were frivolous, arrogant and dandified, following the lead set by the late eighteenth-century Macaronis; other men than Brummell cultivated personal cleanliness – though less fanatically, perhaps; but Brummell, with neither blood nor money, was leader of them all; favourite of the Prince of Wales until he overstepped the mark. Brummell gambled away his modest fortune of £20,000 and his winnings of £36,000. He is said to have won £20,000 one evening and lost £5,000 another.

'He might be frequently met with riding with the Prince of Wales in Hyde Park, or lounging in St James's Street with Prince Esterhazy, who was almost as prominent a figure in the fashionable world. Lord Alvanley, Lord Yarmouth, Lord Fife, and the rest of that most select company of dandies, were sure of being found at a certain hour between White's Club[14] and the shop of Brummell's tailor in Bond Street,' writes another contemporary[15]. In his heyday Brummell patronised everybody.

After the opera, Fanny and Harriette went to Amy's, where Harriette played the piano and Amy danced with Count Benckendorff.

Hearing the Honourable John Ward[16] laugh loudly at his own joke,

Harriette, who disliked him, told him he should bring a footman to do the laughing for him. Well-versed in Latin and Greek, he larded his talk with classical quotations and laughed loudly at his own puns, too learned to be generally understood. His habit of thinking aloud was notorious. He was absent-minded to the point of craziness, though some contemporaries suspected his vagueness was affected and his rudeness calculated. Gronow called him the 'wittiest' and 'most malignant' of men.

Harriette was not unusual in her distaste; Ward was unpopular, though Byron said of him: 'Ward is one of the best-informed men I know and...one of the most agreeable companions.' Lady Charlotte Bury, Lady-in-Waiting to Queen Charlotte, wrote that although he was clever, she could not like him: he looked dirty and 'he has such a sneer in his laugh and is...impious as well as grossly indecent in his conversation.' The Princess of Wales, Caroline of Brunswick, herself of coarse personal habits, complained that he ate like a hog. Nevertheless, Wellington, forming a government in 1828, made him Foreign Secretary.

Julia's lover, Colonel Cotton, was jealous of Brummell's friendship with Julia but, as Harriette observed, Brummell was indifferent to women. Brummell, his mouth full of chicken, urged Harriette on in her mockery of Ward.

'And *look* at that *tie!*' said Brummell fastidiously. He asked Fanny whom he had seen her riding with in the park that morning.

Lord Alvanley answered for her: 'Fanny is a very nice girl, and I wish she wouldn't encourage such people.'

'Who was it, Fanny?' asked Harriette.

'A damned sugar baker,' sneered Alvanley.

'I rode out today,' said Fanny, reddening, 'with a very respectable man of large fortune.'

'Oh yes,' said Alvanley, 'there's a good deal of money to be got in the sugar line.'

Asked his name, Fanny replied, making up a name at random, that it was Mr John Mitchell, who had been at a public school with Lord Alvanley. She had made this up too.

'I don't remember a Mitchell,' said Alvanley, 'but I believe there were a good many grocers admitted at that time.'

Fanny kept up the pretence, saying that Lord Alvanley had been Mitchell's fag and 'distinguished himself by the very high polish he put upon Mr J Mitchell's boots and shoes'. Everybody laughed.

Harriette and Brummell urged Fanny to drop the grocer ' ... and valets who intrude themselves into good society,' added Harriette.

Lord Palmerston[17], Tory member for Newtown, Isle of Wight, later Prime Minister, had just come in.

'My father was a very superior valet,' said Brummell quickly, 'and kept his place, which is more than Palmerston will do.'

Lorne looked as though he wanted to join them, but was afraid of Lady W—'s disapproval. He passed Harriette without acknowledging her as he left, merely hissing through his teeth, 'Aren't you going home, pretty?'

'Do speak louder, Marquis,' said Harriette, in order to pique him. 'I'm not going home for three hours yet; I'm going to Amy's party.'

Lorne smiled beautifully and said, 'At three, then, may I come to you?'

'Yes,' said Harriette, putting her hand in his.

Amy's party was attended by Ward, Luttrell, Nugent, and Benckendorff. Amy wanted to dance the the the waltz[18], the latest craze. She called on a new admirer, Colonel Sydenham, to play his flute for dancing.

After the party Harriette cadged a lift to Argyll House with one of the Russians and Brummell whispered to her: 'You will be Duchess of Argyll, Harriette.' Harriette found Lorne at his door with the key. She asked him why he hadn't gone to Amy's.

He replied coldly that he didn't know her and disliked what he had seen of her. 'She makes so many advances to me!' he added.

Next morning Amy, in a quandary, called on Harriette. Count de Souza Holstein Palmella[19], later Duke of Palmella, was the Portuguese ambassador, wealthy and popular, though swarthy and far from handsome. Portugal was Britain's ally against Napoleon. Amy had arrived in Palmella's barouche, then dismissed him. Harriette said to Amy: 'How terribly rude! I couldn't be rude to such a timid, gentlemanly man as that.'

'Oh, he makes me sick,' said Amy. 'I've come to consult you. I like liberty best,' she explained. 'If I put myself under the protection of anybody, I shan't be allowed to give parties and sit up all night; but then I have my desk full of long bills, without receipts.'

'I thought you were going to marry Benckendorff and go to Russia,' said Harriette.

'Never mind Benckendorff,' said Amy impatiently. 'I want £200 *now*. Palmella wants to have me altogether under his protection. He's rich; but I like Colonel Sydenham best.'

'Sydenham has no money,' said the practical Harriette. 'Palmella seems disposed to do a great deal for you and he is very gentlemanlike; therefore, if a man you must have, my voice is for Palmella!'

'Well,' said Amy. 'I can't stop! I don't much care. Write me a letter directly, to say I consent to enter into the arrangement he has proposed; that is, £200 a month paid in advance, and the use of his horses and carriage.' The letter was sent and Amy took her leave.

Lorne, by this time Duke of Argyll, having inherited in 1806, was about to leave London for Scotland[20] and sometimes he talked of Harriette's going with him. But she was a Londoner, through and through. Lorne had fascinated her and aroused her passion, but he was old enough, she said, to be her father, though in fact he was only ten years older. She resented his continued connexion with Lady W— and had no intention of burying herself in the northern wilderness.

'You won't come with me to Scotland?' pleaded Argyll.

'No,' said Harriette.

Julia, as usual, tells a different story; according to her, Harriette wrote to Lorne:

> MARQUIS — I want to be asked to dinner, merely to see what a Scotchman's house is like. Yours if you please me,
>
> HW

He replied:

> HARRIETTE — A Scotchman's house is like an Englishwoman of my acquaintance – fair without and foul within. Not yours if you tease me,
>
> LORNE

'Really,' he told her later, 'our house is out of repair, and there is no place I could invite you to, except my bedroom.'

'I wouldn't object, if the way to it lay through the family chapel.'

'Our chapel is used only for burials,' retorted Lorne.

It was time for a change. She was getting into debt and the hard-up lover she shared with Lady W— was not much help. She was losing her youth. She went for long walks alone on the river-bank in the autumn chills and fogs, and brooded that she was frittering her life.

She was roused from her gloomy thoughts by a sudden tap on the shoulder from the coarse, red, ungloved hand of her old friend, Lord Frederick Bentinck[21], a younger son of the third Duke of Portland. Lord Frederick held a commission in the 1st Foot Guards.

'My lord, I was just going to drown myself, so please don't leave me here alone,' said Harriette.

Lord Frederick was impervious to this pathetic appeal, saying how much he had to do. His hands on hers were icy.

'At least get yourself some gloves!' said Harriette.

He brushed this aside.

'I only wish you had to listen to the sort of thing I have to deal with every day; everybody wants promotion.' He said he wrote letters to avoid the necessity of talking. 'I hate talking. So, adieu.'

Harriette did not drown herself. She met the Duke of Wellington at the house of a Mrs Porter. Harriette rather fudges this portion of her story. She does

Lorne, after he had become the Duke of Argyll in 1806

not say what she was living on, though she mentions 'my house'. Clearly Mrs Porter's establishment was not respectable. Harriette describes the housekeeper as 'tawdry' and 'well-rouged' and says the Duke was one of Mrs Porter's 'oldest customers'. Mrs Porter had promoted the career of Emma Hart, who – as Lady Hamilton – became the mistress of Horatio Nelson.

A General Walpole having asked to meet her, Harriette agreed and then, getting cold feet, for the General was over sixty, sent him her old nurse covered by a thick veil. Harriette does not say she was actually for sale at Mrs Porter's, but she admits that the Duke – having glimpsed her in the street – asked for her and Mrs Porter told him she had had three applications that month for an introduction to Harriette. He offered £100 to Mrs Porter and £100 to Harriette if a meeting could be arranged[22]. When he arrived at Harriette's house, he took her hand saying, 'Beautiful creature! Where is Lorne?'

'Good gracious!' said Harriette. 'What have you come for, Duke?'

'Your beautiful eyes.'

'Ah, having unpeopled the earth you want to replenish it,' said Harriette in French.

Harriette tells a colourful story of being with Argyll in her bedroom when Wellington banged on the door. Argyll, having told Harriette's manservant not to let anybody in, borrowed her dressing gown and nightcap and, disguised as an old duenna, put on a Cockney voice, pretended to be afraid of burglars and kept Wellington outside in the rain, yelling 'Don't keep me here in the rain, you old blockhead!'

'Sir,' answered Argyll, 'You must please to call out your name, or I daren't come down, robberies being so frequent; it's quite alarming to poor lone women.'

Wellington took off his hat and held up his tired face, rain trickling down his beaky nose. His voice trembling with rage, he roared: 'You old idiot, do you know me now?'

Argyll was enjoying himself.

'Lord, sir! I can't give no guess; and, do you know, sir, them thieves has stolen a new water butt out of our airy … '

'The devil!' cursed Wellington, clenching his teeth and returning to his plain, awkward, neglected wife.

Eventually Argyll, hearing of Wellington's frequent visits, wrote to Harriette:

I'm not quite sure whether I do, or do not love you … but as long as you find pleasure in the society of another, and a hero too, I am well contented to be a mere common mortal, a monkey, or what you will …

Fanny and Julia were dining with Harriette when Amy called. 'What have you done with Palmella?' said Harriette.

'I haven't seen him at all lately,' said Amy, playing with the fringe of her shawl.

'Did you send the letter I wrote for you?'

'Yes.'

'And did he send you the £200?'

'At once, and a letter full of the deepest gratitude,' said Amy complacently.

'And where's the dear little man now?'

'God knows!' cried Amy. 'I've turned him away ever since. Sydenham has been telling me I'm too beautiful to throw myself away on Palmella.'

'What about the £200?'

'I've spent it.'

Notes to Chapter Three

1. Page 30: *Clara Gazul* (vol 3, 178).

2. Page 30: *Confessions*, p55.

3. Page 30: Between 1670 and 1857 there were only 325 divorces in England.

4. Page 31: This took place before Harriette had met Julia, who was Lord Proby's cousin. Julia's uncle was John Joshua, first Earl of Carysfort (1751–1828), only son of Sir John Proby, later first Baron Carysfort. John Joshua had succeeded to the barony in 1772 and been raised to an earldom in 1789. Cultivated and poetical, Lord Carysfort was from 1800 until 1802 Minister Plenipotentiary in Berlin.

5. Page 31: *Confessions*, pp 173, 53. Messalina was the sexually insatiable wife of the Roman emperor Claudius, who had her executed.

6. Page 31: George Nugent-Grenville, Baron Nugent (1788–1850), later an MP. He supported the enfranchisement of Roman Catholics.

7. Page 32: Count Woronzow (otherwise Count Semen Vorontzov) was appointed Russian ambassador to England in 1784 and stayed until 1806. Upon retirement he settled in London and died in 1832, aged 89. His daughter Caroline became the second wife of the eleventh Earl of Pembroke in 1808.

8. Page 32: Henry Luttrell (1765?–1849?). Harriette describes him as 'our father confessor' in London and in Paris and says he was 'methodistical'. This adjective may have been an innnuendo: in Byron's circle, 'methodism' was a euphemism for homosexuality. Luttrell was safe, Harriette felt, in that he was 'not attracted' to her – nor, it may be assumed, to any other woman. Byron valued him for his epigrammatic conversation; Greville found him 'somewhat too epigrammatic, but very witty'. Samuel Rogers said of him: 'No one could slide in a brilliant thing with greater readiness'. Luttrell was to publish in 1820 a once-famous poem, *Advice to Julia: A Letter in Rhyme*, which reached a third edition by 1822.

9. Page 32: *Reminiscences*, p184.

10. Page 32: William Arden, second baron, 1789–1849. After the *Memoirs* were published, Lord Alvanley agreed that Harriette had caught his tone accurately (Sir Walter Scott, *Journal*, 9 December 1825). Alvanley inherited his title in 1804. In 1831 he married Arabella, daughter of the Duke of Cleveland, but had no children.

11. Page 33: Thomas Creevey, MP (1768–1838). Educated at Queens' College, Cambridge, he was called to the bar in 1794.

12. Page 33: Thomas Raikes, *Journal*, 22 May 1835. The same story about Alvanley appears in the *Table Talk* of Samuel Rogers. Raikes (1777-1848) was a friend of Brummell's from their Eton days and, like Brummell, played for high stakes at Crockford's and White's. He was a hanger-on of the dandy circle.

Alvanley's urbanity is illustrated by another anecdote: 'Lord Kinnaird and Lord Alvanley were playing at whist, when the former scolded the latter in the most violent manner. Lord Alvanley got up, saying very quietly, "Not being blessed with your Lordship's angelic temper, I shall retire for fear of losing mine".' (Harriet, Countess Granville, to Lady Georgiana Morpeth, 1 January 1819).

13. Page 34: The Duke of York, who died in 1826, was brother to the Prince of Wales. The Duchess died in 1820. Raikes writes of Oatlands that it was 'the only existing retreat of correct mannners and high breeding'. He says that Lords Alvanley and Worcester helped Brummell after his decline into poverty (Raikes, *Journal*, 12 September 1835), though shady dealing was suspected (see Chapter 12).

14. Page 34: White's, an exclusive and expensive gentlemen's club. Gronow says; 'White's was most difficult of entry: its list of members comprised nearly all the noble names of Great Britain. The politics of White's Club were then decidedly Tory. It was here that play was carried on to an extent which made many ravages in large fortunes … ' (*Reminiscences*, p58). Gronow instances a win of £200,000 at whist.

15. Page 34: The Honourable Grantley F Berkeley, *My Life and Recollections*, (vol 3, 43). 'All the world watched Brummell to imitate him … ' (Gronow, *Reminiscences*, p56). Brummell once said to the Duke of Bedford, feeling a lapel delicately with his finger; 'Bedford, do you call this thing a coat?' The story is fictionalised by the contemporary novelist Edward Bulwer-Lytton:

> ' … Look at this coat, for instance,' and Sir Willoughby Townshend made a dead halt, that we might admire his garment the more accurately.
> 'Coat!' said Russelton, with an appearance of … surprise, and taking hold of the collar, suspiciously, by the finger and thumb; 'coat, Sir Willoughby! Do you call this thing a coat?' (*Pelham*, Chapter 32).

In 1829, the year after *Pelham* was published to considerable acclaim, Harriette wrote from Paris to the author saying that she had got to the end of it, though she did not like it much. She confessed that all her life she disliked reading, except for Shakespeare's plays. This contradicts claims made in the *Memoirs* that she read Racine and Voltaire and decided to 'study like mad'.

16. Page 34: John William Ward (1781–1833), first Earl and fourth Viscount Dudley and ninth Baron Ward. Lord Glenbervie noted that he 'dislikes and despises, or (which is in worse taste still) affects to dislike and despise the writings of Shakespeare'. Ward was bullied and neglected as a child, which might account for some of his peculiarities. George Thomas Keppel, Earl of Albemarle, records that Ward had 'two voices, a gruff

bass and a high treble'. Dining with King William IV, Ward was heard to comment on the culinary falling off since the days of George IV, 'What a change – cold patés and hot champagne!' (Albermarle, *Fifty Years of My Life*, vol 2, 294). Lord Dudley opposed the Parliamentary changes which resulted in the1832 Reform Bill. He eventually became quite mad, driving to the house of a married mistress, Sarah, Lady Lyndhurst, and begging that a clergyman should be sent for at once to baptize her second daughter, 'who is near four years old and whom scandal ascribes to him' (Le Marchant's diary 10 April 1832). Ward was locked up. He appears in Harriette's novel *Clara Gazul* as Lord Dolittle and in *Pelham* as Lord Vincent.

17. Page 35: Henry John Temple, third Viscount Palmerston (1784–1865), later Foreign Secretary, Home Secretary and Prime Minister.

18. Page 36: The waltz, derived from the Austrian *Ländler*, was invented in Vienna in the late 1780s, and swept through France, but did not arrive in England till about 1812. The Duke of Argyll married in 1810. Harriette's narrative, here and elsewhere, blends various separate occasions and is only apparently sequential. The tunes arrived before the new way of dancing did, and lessons in the new dance were advertised. Until 1814 or so, old dances were performed to the new tunes. Lord Byron wrote a long poem, in which he rhymes 'waltz' with 'salts', on the new dance:

> Morals and minuets, virtue and her stays,
> And tell-tale powder, all have had their days,

he says, summing up social trends:

> Endearing Waltz! To thy more melting tune
> Bow Irish jig and ancient rigadoon.
> Scotch reels, avaunt! and country-dance forego
> Your future claims to each fantastic toe!
> Waltz – Waltz alone – both legs and arms demands,
> Liberal of feet, and lavish of her hands;
> Hands which may freely range in public sight
> Where ne'er before – but 'pray put out the light' …
> The breast thus publicly resign'd to man,
> In private may resist him – if it can.

The poet suggests that such heated intimacy on the dance floor is likely to lead to promiscuity. As Byron's poem emphasises, the 'seductive' and even 'voluptuous' waltz was considered exciting, even immoral, because it offered unprecedented opportunities for grasping a partner round the waist, instead of leading her by the hand. When clasping one's partner on the dance floor became the fashion, mothers forbade it.

19. Page 36: Palmella (1786–1850) later represented Portugal at Queen Victoria's coronation in 1837.

20. Page 36: The Duke of Argyll entertained lavishly at Inverary, known as the 'Castle of Indolence' because everybody stayed up so late. Elizabeth, Lady Holland mentions hearing Tom Sheridan still at billiards at seven-thirty in the morning (*Journal*, 8 September 1807). Gronow lists Argyll among the dandies.

21. Page 37: According to Julia, Harriette frequently pleaded poverty to Lord Frederick Bentinck: ' ... not a fire in the grate at home, nor a chop in the larder ... no sooner [did] he put a note in her hand than she squandered it on trinkets, laughing at his credulity' (*Confessions*, p88). Lord Glenbervie wrote in his *Journal*: 'Lord Frederick Bentinck seems good-natured, as all the Bentincks seem' (17 April 1818). Lord Frederick married Lady Mary Lowther on 16 September 1820.

22. Page 38: Julia says Harriette paid Mrs Porter 100 guineas to be introduced to Wellington, who never refused her £15 or £20 (*Confessions*, p115). Harriette never admits that their relation was sexual, though she leaves us in no doubt that Mrs Porter's was not a respectable house. In *Clara Gazul* we read that a Madame D'Eperlan is 'the most notorious procuress in London' (vol 2, 116); Mrs Porter may be intended.

Greville wrote later:

> The Duke was a good-natured, but not an amiable man; he had no tenderness in his disposition ... His nature was hard, and he does not appear to have had any real affection for anybody, man or woman ... Domestic enjoyment he never possessed, and, as his wife was intolerable to him, though he always kept on decent terms with her, at least, ostensibly, he sought the pleasure of women's society in a variety of capricious liaisons, from which his age took all scandal ... In his younger days he was extremely addicted to gallantry, and had great success with women (*Diary*, 18 September 1852).

4

TRUE LOVE AND BLACK PUDDING

Amy changed her name and abode, calling herself Mrs Sydenham. She continued to give parties, but Colonel Sydenham imposed a 3am curfew. Fanny moved in with Julia, paying half the rent.

Julia was desperate for money. Colonel Cotton, with nine legitimate children, could not afford to support his five illegitimate ones by Julia. She soon gave birth to their sixth. Julia applied repeatedly to her grand relatives, who were mean with money but lavish with reproaches. Harriette and Fanny urged Julia to forget Cotton and find someone with means. Julia told them how she had been seduced by Cotton on a stone staircase at Hampton Court – which sounds uncomfortable. It was otherwise difficult for the lovers to meet.

'My bedroom,' said Julia, 'was next to mamma's. My sister always shared our mother's bed, but kept her clothes in my room. One day Cotton said to me, "Suppose I were to conceal myself under your bed?"

'"My mamma always comes into my room to kiss me goodnight."

'"I'll wait till everybody's gone."

'"How will you put up with being under a bed for three or four hours?"

'"I could put up with anything!"

'"But my sister uses my room to dress and undress."

'"I'll be silent as the grave," said Cotton. Fancy him, then, safely hidden under my bed, with my sister and I undressing together, me conscious of being watched by an adoring romantic lover, my sister carelessly washing, splashing and rattling and talking about her pimples and her warts!'

They all laughed. 'Now, Amy, it's your turn to confess,' said Harriette. 'How did you come by all those £100 notes when you were with poor Madden, and I was a good little girl at home?'

'If you must know, Hart Davis used to pat me, and they came from him.'

'Pat you?'

'On the arm, like this,' said Amy.

'Was that all?'

'That was all, I assure you. "A-a-amy! A-a-amy!", he used to say, drawing down his bushy eyebrows, and patting my arm, "does that feel nice?" I told him quite fiercely that it didn't, but one day I wanted £100, so when he began asking me the usual question I said, "Yes, thank you; I think it does feel ra-a-ther nice!" And whenever I admitted it, which I did only rarely, it got me £100.'

'Do pray send your patting men to me,' said Julia.

Wellington came often, though Harriette found him less than entertaining. In the evenings, when he wore his broad red ribbon, he looked 'like a ratcatcher', or at other times shabby, like 'the apothecary in *Romeo and Juliet*'. Harriette's imagination was preoccupied with a stranger, neither young nor brightly dressed, who walked a Newfoundland dog. He did not strike her as handsome, but his pale expressive – expressive being a favourite word of hers – beauty stole upon her by degrees and played a starring role in her romantic fantasies. She went out one evening on impulse on one of her moody walks in Hyde Park, and saw him between two large elm trees, on his horse. Their eyes met.

Harriette went quietly home. Fanny warned her not to make a fool of herself. Although Fanny scolded her, Harriette was busy building castles in the air. She was pining to touch the handsome stranger's horse or his dog: 'I should be half wild with joy,' she told Fanny, who mocked her for talking nonsense.

One evening when the Three Graces were at the opera, Harriette saw her handsome, sad-faced, dark-skinned stranger again. Harriette excitedly pointed him out to short-sighted Julia, who quizzed him through her eye-glass. Julia said she knew him and that he had jilted a friend of hers, now Lady Conyngham[1]. Julia identified Harriette's mysterious stranger as 'John Ponsonby, who is supposed to be the handsomest man in England; but he must now be forty, if not more[2]'. Harrette, enchanted by his 'godlike head, mouth of perfect loveliness, and peculiarly intellectual beauty' declared she was in love with him, and Fanny, who had a keen sense of the ridiculous, teased her.

'What chance can you have?' asked Julia. 'He's married to the loveliest creature – Lord Jersey's youngest daughter. He lives in Curzon Street.' Lady Frances Ponsonby had been Lady Elizabeth-Frances Villiers, daughter of the fourth Earl of Jersey. The portrait of her by John Opie, in private hands, shows her as indeed exquisitely beautiful in a classically perfect way.

Ponsonby became Harriette's obsession. She passed his house fifty times, stared at his footmen, and brooded on his door-knocker because he must have touched it. She shivered when she passed him in the street.

George Brummell wrote her affected, gushing letters. Lord Frederick Bentinck gave her kindly advice and shook his head over her morals. One day he was admiring himself in her looking glass, ungloved as usual. He had a new pair of leather breeches[3], and wanted to see how they fitted. Brummell arrived, and Harriette told him Lord Frederick wanted his opinion.

'Come here, Fred Bentinck!' said Brummell. 'But there is only one man on earth who can make leather breeches!'

'Mine were made by a man in the Haymarket,' said Bentinck proudly. He rarely treated himself to new clothes.

'My dear fellow, take them off directly!' commanded Brummell.

'I hope he'll do no such thing!' cried Harriette.

'They only came this morning, and I thought they were rather neat,' said Fred Bentinck, looking anxiously at himself in the glass.

'Bad knees, my good fellow! Bad knees!' said Brummell, with a shrug.

Wellington told Harriette she ought to get married. She found him 'uphill work', since he had no small-talk and did not indulge in the flirtatious badinage she was used to. She decided he was 'worse than Lord Craven', though he was generous with his money. Harriette continued to haunt Curzon Street, though John and Frances Ponsonby were out of town.

Eventually a note soliciting Harriette's acquaintance arrived from him. Harriette, delirious with joy, replied that for five months she had thought of little else but Ponsonby. She tells us that her happiness in continuing their correspondence was 'the purest, the most exalted, and the least allied to sensuality' of her life. By mutual consent they met in the park not to speak but only to look at each other. When he first came to her house, she burst into tears of joy.

'My dear, dear little Harriette,' said Ponsonby, drawing her towards him and passing his arm gently about her slender waist. They talked together all night, her head on his shoulder. He confessed he had been watching her long before they met. He told her he had seen her with Argyll and for several days afterwards could think of nothing else: 'At the opera I heard all the fine young men talking about you. Though you didn't see me, I was always looking at you and trying to hear some one talk about you. When we met in Hyde Park, there was something so natural and unaffected, and wild, about your manner, that I began to forget your notoriety,' he said. They parted without a kiss. The next night he talked for half an hour and said to her: 'Do you know what I'm proudest of in the world and which, poor as I am, upon my honour, I would not exchange at this moment for a hundred thousand pounds?'

'No.'

'I'll tell you – my place in your heart and your arms, this evening.' He put his arms round her slim waist and her lips were almost touching his. She writes:

Ponsonby's cheek was now tinged with the glowing blush of passion; yet he turned from my kiss like a spoiled child.

'No,' said Ponsonby, shaking his head, 'I have a thousand things to tell you.'

'I cannot listen to one of them,' said I faintly, and our lips met in one long, long delicious kiss! so sweet! so ardent! that it seemed to draw the life's warm current from my youthful heart, to reanimate his with all its wildest passion.

And then! – yes, and then, as Sterne says —

And then — and then — and then — and then — and then we parted.

The next day, at past three o'clock, Fanny found me in bed.

Ponsonby and Harriette met every evening for a week, rarely separating before five or six in the morning. Harriette was convinced that he sharpened her wits and brought out the best in her. A married man, he could not be seen visiting her house.

About a week after he first visited her, Harriette was expecting him at about midnight. She went to bed and fell asleep. Harriette had stamina, but was fond of her sleep. When she woke, the morning sun was shining through the curtains. Her first thoughts were always of Ponsonby and she was disappointed that her maid had not woken her as requested. He had given her a little watch which she always placed under her pillow at night. She felt for it and was astonished to find a magnificent chain attached. Rubbing her eyes, she was even more surprised to find a beautiful pearl ring on her finger. Now she was fully awake, she spotted a slip of paper with a pencilled message in Ponsonby's elegant small script. It said, in French: 'Sleep on, dear child: I love you too dearly to disturb you.'

She was delighted with this evidence of affectionate consideration. On the other hand she was exasperated at missing him. How could she have been so stupid as not to wake when his hand was under her pillow? She rang the bell and asked how long Ponsonby had stayed the previous night.

'Over an hour,' was the reply.

Kissing the watch and chain, Harriette was overwhelmed with love and gratitude. He was the first man in her experience to sacrifice his own pleasure to her comfort. She adored his gentleness, his shyness until he had a drink inside him, his musical speaking voice and his manly beauty. Harriette was not alone in admiring Ponsonby; he was famous for his good looks, which had saved him from being hanged in Paris during the Revolution. Women in the mob had cut him down, saying he was too handsome to die. Ponsonby was not such a virtuoso in bed as Lorne had been, but Harriette was convinced she had found true love. With it came unprecedented ecstasy for her. She adored everything about him, in particular his voice. He called her his 'angelic Harriette', told her he had never felt such a tenderness of affection for any woman, combining all a father might feel for a daughter with the wildest passion his first youth had been capable of. Ponsonby was a foot fetishist, and went everywhere with one of Harriette's small shoes in his pocket, so that the new ones he constantly bought for her would fit.

Ponsonby was an Irish peer, second baron and later first Viscount Ponsonby of Imokilly. His melancholy had been caused by the lingering death of his father. William Ponsonby, a younger son, had been ennobled as first Baron Ponsonby for public service in Ireland on March 13 1806, but died later the same year. John Ponsonby, now a lord, and not just an Honourable, had come back from his Irish estates looking handsomer than ever in his deep mourning. Like most of his circle, he was a Whig politician, friend of Charles James Fox, and Harriette did her best to read history and Parliamentary debates, and decided to support the Opposition because Ponsonby was a member of it, though it went against the grain of her 'aristocratical prejudices'; her sympathies were with the Tories[4]. Having a 'sneaking kindness', however, for her king, she decided she could not become – as so many Whigs were – a republican; she could only be politically neutral.

When Ponsonby visited his Irish estates again Harriette was disconsolate in his absence. She went to the country for a fortnight and asked her landlady for a quiet comfortable room to study in. Harriette elegantly mocks her own resolution of becoming 'clever and learned at the shortest notice'. She considered Shakespeare was too entertaining to count as study. She decided to start with ancient history.

'The Greeks employed me for two whole days, and the Romans six more: I took down notes ... I then read *Charles the Twelfth*, by Voltaire ... then, Rousseau's *Confessions* ... Racine's *Tragedies* ... and Boswell's *Life of Johnson*.. I allowed myself only ten minutes for dinner.'

She was saved from studying herself to death under this regime by a visit from her mother. Mrs Dubochet was worried about Harriette's younger sister, Sophia, who was being pursued by the debauched Lord Deerhurst[5]. Despite a reputation as a wit, a match according to Gronow for Alvanley, he was fond of running after pretty women in the street, and was dirty in his personal habits. He had been writing to Sophia, then thirteen, and had made her presents of cheap jewellery in boxes from Love and Wirgman, expensive jewellers.

Amy gave parties but lived cheaply between times on toad-in-the-hole [sausages in batter] and black pudding [blood sausage]. She sent Sophia,who was beginning to give herself airs, to the pork-butcher's to buy a pound of black pudding, food of the poor. It was wrapped only in a scrap of *The Times* and Sophia had to hold her purchase by the middle, feeling humiliated at walking down South Audley Street with this greasy blood sausage, afraid of spoiling her new frock. Suddenly she saw Lord Deerhurst approaching and bundled the pudding into the folds of her skirt, wishing pockets had not gone out of fashion. Deehurst held out his hand to her, so she threw the pudding down behind her to take it.

An Irish labourer picked it up and called after her, giving it a wipe with his dirty ragged sleeve. He held it out to her, reminding her she had dropped it. Deerhurst burst out laughing and Sophia, overcome with shame and rage, denied having dropped anything and ran away back to Amy empty-handed.

Sophia was already out to advance herself; she spoke in shooting parlance of 'levelling a peer' and 'winging a duke' even of 'hamstringing an alderman' – a vocabulary culled from the sporting peers who were Harriette's admirers. Deerhurst was a friend of Alvanley.

Soon afterwards,'Sophia is off! Sophia is off!' cried Harriette's sisters. She

*Sophia drops the black pudding and is not pleased
at having it rescued when she meets Lord Deerhurst*

had run away with Lord Deerhurst. Mrs Dubochet was too crushed to act. Harriette sent a note to Deerhurst and he brought Sophia back, weeping and swearing that he and Sophia had spent the night in mere conversation. Harriette was convinced that her youngest sister went away with Lord Deerhurst 'as innocent as an infant of the nature of seduction and its consequences'. Sophia's family threatened him with the law unless he made her an allowance. Their only legal claim on Deerhurst, they discovered, was that her parents had lost her domestic services. There was at that time no legal age of consent and girls often married at fourteen. After some months, Deerhurst said that if Sophia stayed with him, he would settle £300 a year on her; if she were unfaithful, this would be reduced to one hundred. He hired cheap lodgings for her and sent her six bottles of red-currant wine, saying it was better for her health than foreign wine. Sophia grew to hate him and his habit of getting dressed without washing first.

One day he took her and Harriette out for 'dinner' – fried bacon and eggs in a country pub that stank of tobacco. On the way back, he galloped his horses at a turnpike to avoid paying a twopenny toll and got into a fight with the collector, who grabbed his whip and called Deerhurst a 'damned blackguard'. The whip broke and Deerhurst jumped out of the curricle, leaving the women, who were not dressed for walking, to control two spirited horses. He stripped off his coat and was soon fighting with a fat, dirty member of the proletariat, while a crowd gathered and cheered them on with 'You a lord? Go to it, my lord.'

Deerhurst followed the Regency fashion for cultivating prizefighters and among his associates were the famous champions Tom Cribb and 'Gentleman' Jackson[6], who had given him boxing lessons. He was persuaded to pay his twopence by the Honourable Arthur Upton, who was passing. Upton, who was one of Amy's lovers, got a villager to hold the horses. Deerhurst returned, bruised and bleeding, to Harriette and Sophia, as if nothing had happened, leaving his opponent black and blue, with no compensation but his lawful twopence. The mob hissed and hooted their disapproval of 'rum lords' who cheated a poor man out of twopence and then stopped to fight in the road.

One night when the Three Graces were in their opera box, the first man who joined them there was Fred Lamb, who appeared delighted to see Harriette.

'When did you come to town?' she asked.

'This morning,' Fred answered, 'and I called on you; but you were either out or denied to me.'

'I passed the morning in my little library,' she answered.

'You've made me very wretched,' he whispered, pressing her hand violently.

'I didn't intend to.'

He begged her to 'throw away two whole days in the country' with him. He suggested the Cock Inn at Sutton.

'What shall we do there?' said Harriette, frankly puzzled.

'Get married?' suggested Julia hopefully.

'Married!' exploded Fred Lamb. 'From my heart and soul, I pity the man who ever hopes to attach you, Harriette. You have the knack of torturing those who love you. Why didn't you tell me that you didn't intend to receive me?'

'I meant well,' she said, sighing. She reflected there was no pleasure in being loved by those she could not love in return.

'If you were my wife, by God, I'd have murdered you long ago,' said Fred Lamb; he was only half joking.

Harriette flippantly promised to become steady and settle down at fifty.

Fred said that by then she would have changed her mind.

Lord Molyneux came into her box. She always made a point of flirting with him, as she did with Luttrell, because they were not attracted to her. She congratulated Molyneux on his white silk stockings – then going out of fashion.

She pretended to be 'stark, staring mad for' him.

'I'm off,' said Fred Lamb.

Julia, who had a soft spot for Fred, begged him to stay. He persuaded Harriette to go out with him. Harriette, accompanied by her maid, was soon in her travelling dress and on the road to Sutton. Fred was waiting for her. While their meal was being cooked, he read poetry to her in the sing-song way that had recently become fashionable and which irritated her.

They had an excellent dinner, but when the waiter brought candles and it looked as though she was expected to stay the night, Harriette's courage failed her. She did not like Fred Lamb. She tried to tell herself that since she had already lived under his protection, one more night would not make much difference. If she left him now, he would probably feel ill-used and become her bitter enemy. But the idea of spending the night with Fred Lamb was repugnant. Their relationship had ended several years previously and in between she had been the mistress of Lorne and the devoted lover of Ponsonby. But she was afraid of Fred. Pale with terror, she told him she had to get back to London. She didn't want to hurt him, she said, and if she had given the wrong impression, she was sorry. But feelings couldn't always be controlled. Fred's pride was hurt, but on this occasion he behaved like a gentleman, ordering her carriage and taking her home. They parted at her door with friendly politeness.

Walking one day in Hyde Park with 'Poodle' Byng of the Foreign Office, so called because of his tight white curls, Harriette noticed a beautiful young woman in an elegant little carriage and was told it was 'that most lovely creature Fanny Ponsonby, whom we're all sighing and dying for'. She had perfect features and big dark eyes and looked about eighteen. Harriette told Ponsonby she had seen his wife and admired her. Ponsonby solemnly told his mistress that he would die rather than destroy his wife's peace. Harriette had to accept, as the mistresses of married men often have to, that she took second place, and did her best to persuade herself that she didn't mind too much.

An acquaintance called Matthew Lee had told Harriette in 1808 that Frances Ponsonby was 'a sweet-tempered child, but not at all clever', adding that men soon grew tired of the Villiers women, for all their beauty. Gentle Lady Ponsonby was profoundly deaf, owing to scarlet fever. She had first met Ponsonby when she was fourteen. During her illness shortly afterwards, her waist-length hair had been all cut off[7]. She often took off her lace cap to raise a laugh: or perhaps she knew that even shorn she was lovely as ever.

'Lord Ponsonby felt the deepest interest, admiration and pity for her. He might have done better,' said Matthew. 'Her ladyship is good and will do as she is bid; but besides her deafness, her understanding is neither bright nor lively. Lord Ponsonby shows her the sort of indulgence and tenderness which a child requires; but he must seek for a companion elsewhere.' She amused herself, he added, with a mouse she had tamed by feeding it with crumbs, and did not care for society. She had been married for five years, having married in 1803, and was still only twenty.

Harriette was twenty-two, at the peak of her attractiveness. Her bold sexuality and pert witticisms must have been stimulating to her lover, a refreshing contrast to his timid, childish bride, beautiful but insipid. Often, after spending the early part of the evening together, they would take a cab to the House of Lords, and Harriette would sit waiting in it half the night, just for a goodnight kiss and the pleasure of driving with him to his own door at 12 Upper Brook Street. Meanwhile Lady Ponsonby during the long evenings relied for company and entertainment on her pet mouse.

Notes to Chapter Four

1. Page 45: The Marchioness of Conyngham was mistress to the Prince of Wales, later King George IV. Mrs Charles Arbuthnot's *Diary* (7 March 1820) records that the Duke of Wellington told her of a diplomatic document which reported the news that the Prince Regent (then fifty-eight) had deserted Lady Hertford, mother of Fanny Dubochet's friend Lord Yarmouth, and sixty years old, for Lady Conyngham, then fifty. Lord Ponsonby had remained on good, probably intimate, terms with Lady Conyngham, to the irritation of the King.

Greville's *Diary* (31 July 1831) says:

> Harriet [*sic*] Wilson, at the time of her connection with Lord Ponsonby, got hold of some of Lady Conyngham's letters to him, and she wrote to Ponsonby, threatening, unless he gave her a large sum, to come to England and publish everything she could. This produced dismay among all the parties, and they wanted to get Ponsonby away and silence the woman … Ponsonby was sent to Buenos Ayres forthwith and the letters were bought up.

2. Page 45: Harriette had sent a copy of her *Memoirs* to Lady Ponsonby from Paris, her pious resolution about not wounding her lover's wife forgotten, but finding this act of spite ignored she threatened to publish Lady Conyngham's letters. King George IV, afraid of scandal, consulted Sir William Knighton, his physician and confidential adviser, and the appointment was arranged in 1826, the year after the *Memoirs* were published. The bargain was made and Harriette got her hush-money. Ponsonby was known in society as 'handsome Ponsonby' (Elizabeth, Lady Holland, *Journal*, 30 May 1800). Greville gives us a late glimpse, when Ponsonby was Ambassador to Turkey:

> Lord Ponsonby is a most remarkable-looking man for his age, which is seventy-two or seventy-three. He exhibits no signs of old age, and is extremely agreeable (*Diary*, 5 October 1842).

A sketch of him by Henry Bone survives in the National Portrait Gallery, showing him to have been handsome indeed, with regular features. Ponsonby was a cousin of Lady Caroline Lamb. He was made a Viscount in 1839. His wife Frances was a sister of Argyll's Duchess – formerly Lady Caroline Villiers, later Lady Paget – who married Argyll as her second husband. The daughters of George Villiers, fourth Earl of Jersey, were all famous for their good looks.

3. Page 45: Pronounced, according to Walker, as 'britchiz'. This pronunciation is still preferable to 'breaches', often heard today.

4. Page 48: The word 'Conservative' was not used in a political context till 1834.

5. Page 48: Viscount Deerhurst, later tenth Earl of Coventry (1784–1843), an eccentric

who died insane. The Honourable Grantley F Berkeley, who knew Deerhurst from boyhood, writes of a scene in the 1830s involving threats to Lord Coventry by an injured husband: 'I found Lord Coventry … in a strange, drivelling state of rage, jealousy, friendliness and tears' (*My Life and Recollections*, vol 2, 137).

6. Page 50: John ('Gentleman') Jackson (1769–1845) was the most popular teacher of boxing. He is credited with giving the sport its scientific principles. Tom Moore, the poet, in his *Memoirs*, wrote that Jackson 'made more than a thousand a year by teaching sparring'. Among his pupils was Byron who, when chided for keeping company with a pugilist, insisted that Jackson's manners were 'infinitely superior to those of the Fellows of the college whom I meet at the High Table' and referred to him in 'Hints from Horace':

> And men unpractised in exchanging knocks
> Must go to Jackson ere they dare to box.

The Honourable Grantley F Berkeley recalled Jackson at Brighton as a child: 'He … taught me to use my then very small fists, placing me between his knees and holding up his huge palms for me to hit at' (*My Life and Recollections*, vol 1, p73). Jackson married a widow who kept the Cock Inn at Sutton, who stipulated that he should give up fighting; her husband's presence made the inn famous. Jackson was buried in a grand tomb with caryatids in Brompton cemetery.

7. Page 51: It was the custom until the twentieth century to cut off the hair of a woman who became ill, especially of 'fever'; it was a popular belief that the growth of hair took all her strength; compare the Biblical legend of Samson (Judges 13–16). Lady Frances's illness may have left her sterile as well as deaf. She had no children. Possibly her husband preferred to sleep not with her but with others.

5

A WOMAN SCORNED

After several happy years with Ponsonby, during which he paid her rent and other expenses, Harriette one evening thought he seemed sad. She told him so, but he denied it, insisting he was in fact more than usually cheerful. Harriette wondered whether he might be unwell:

'Your hands are feverish.'

'Yes, that must be it,' said Ponsonby, bursting into laughter. 'I'm going to die. Would you be sorry?' Taking her piquant face between his hands, he kissed her gently on the forehead, sighed, and looked lingeringly into her eyes.

'I won't ask you that. I'm sure you would.' He sighed again, then picked up some paper and began to write, shielding the sheet with his hand.

'What are you writing?' she asked curiously.

'Private business,' he said.

Probably he's writing something for me, thought Harriette. After all, he was in her house. Unwilling to interrupt him, she sat down at her piano. Perhaps he's going to keep his promise and allow me two hundred pounds a year, she thought to herself. But she knew he was heavily in debt and decided that if he made any such reckless offer she would nobly refuse. Ponsonby sealed the letter and put it in his pocket. He looked at his watch and jumped to his feet.

'I must go!' he said agitatedly. 'Who would have thought it could be so late?'

'Must you go home already?'

'I don't have to go home, but I do have to go to the House of Lords, though I can't bear the thought of losing your company. You may be right; I am feeling a little down this evening. Will you come as far as the House with me in a hackney coach?'

'Of course I will,' said Harriette. 'Please let me wait for you outside. I don't care if I have to wait all night. You'll come out eventually and we can drive back to your house together.'

'You are so sweet,' said Ponsonby heavily. They drove to the house and Harriet waited outside in the cab. After half an hour he came out and smiled at her. 'We shall be sitting late,' he said. 'I can't bear the thought of your hanging about all night.'

'No, honestly, I don't mind waiting for you,' said Harriette. 'I'll stay here till you come back.' I would wait for this man for ever, she thought; what difference can a couple of hours make?'

It was dawn when he left the House. He looked awful – ill and exhausted. Harriette hadn't seen him in such a state since his father's death. He gave her no greeting, but kissed her greedily over and over again. They drove towards the home he shared with his wife, now in Upper Brook Street.

'I can see how tired you are, you poor darling!' murmured Harriette, stroking his face. 'If only I could stay with you always and take care of you for ever.'

Ponsonby did not respond. After several minutes' silence he took the letter he had written earlier that evening from his pocket.

'I have a letter for you,' he said, holding it out.

'No, I won't accept it!' cried Harriette. 'I can guess what's in it. It's the allowance you promised me, isn't it?'

His handsome face was impassive.

'Read the letter,' he pressed.

She took it from his hand and tore it into little pieces, tossing them out of the carriage window. Unconsciously she had feared the worst and her instinct had been right. She never saw Ponsonby again. A curt note in the mail ended the affair for ever. He used the traditional excuse that his wife had found out, though she had known for a good while[1].

Harriette took to her bed for several weeks. Her anguish was unbearable and she suffered a mental and physical breakdown. Writing a dozen or more years later, she gives us every detail of her trauma, never forgotten. Her first thought was to throw herself out of the window, but it wasn't high enough. Fatuously she told herself she would have been happy as Ponsonby's slave with only a smile as a week's reward; she even got religion for a while. Besotted, she haunted the street outside Ponsonby's house, and sheltered under a porch from the icy wind.

A poor shivering girl joined her, coughing. She was neatly dressed and unpainted. Poor thing, thought Harriette: perhaps the girl had to prostitute herself to drunken and unfeeling strangers, in order to live. What am I, Harriette asked herself, that I should turn my back on a sister in affliction?

'What are you doing out here with that dreadful cough?' said Harriette.

'I'm homeless. They've been and turned me into the streets because I'm too ill to earn a shilling.' She had a spasm of coughing as she spoke and Harriette saw she was dying.

Harriette asked her, with unintentional irony: 'Good God! How could you degrade yourself in such a way! What hard labour would not have been preferable at the beginning?' The girl fainted.

Harriette took her home in a cab. The girl told Harriette she had been a respectable nursery-maid. Her young man delayed marrying her, waiting – so he said – for his father's consent. He was actually married and father of three children. She left her job and took another, but was so visibly morose that she was sacked.

'I got into bad company and, having lost my character as well as my health, I have, for the last four months, been reduced to eating the bread of sin.'

Harriette, using influence, got the girl admitted to hospital. Obsessed with her own grief, Harriette went back to haunting Upper Brook Street where Ponsonby now lived. She told herself she could die happy if she could only get a glimpse of him again. One evening as she wandered she got caught in a storm and was soaked in the rain. She sat down on a doorstep, her elegant clothes bedraggled.

After Ponsonby deserted her, Harriette took to haunting Upper Brook Street, where he lived, obsessively hoping for a glimpse of him, but she was always disappointed

A man's voice broke into her reverie. 'What are you doing sitting there in this weather?'

Drearily she looked up. An old man with a long white beard and a black hat and coat was looking down at her, concern on his kindly old face.

He took her hand gently. 'You poor young thing!' he said, shaking his head. 'God bless my soul, you have much fever. You are ill! Don't be afraid of a poor old Jew. Tell me how I can help you.'

'Yes, I am very ill,' faltered Harriette, struggling to speak calmly. 'If – perhaps – you could get me a hackney coach, that would be very kind.'

The old man found a cab and helped her into it. What delicacy, she thought – he didn't ask me any questions. She almost collapsed again at the door of her house. Her housekeeper was shocked at her wild, dishevelled appearance and sent for Dr Bain, Harriette's (fashionable and expensive) physician, at once. Dr Bain was a friend of the Sheridan family. He diagnosed a high fever and prescribed rest. She confessed her trouble to him and begged him to let her have a writing desk set before her. Reluctantly he allowed her maid to bring one and administered a strong opiate. Her brain whirled with futile messages to her lost lover and despite the sedative she slept only fitfully before six o'clock the next morning. Then she fell into a drugged sleep lasting eight hours.

When she woke, she found Dr Bain and her beloved sister Fanny at her bedside. The doctor told Fanny that Harriette's illness was caused by emotional turmoil, so severe that bloodletting[2] was necessary.

After five days in bed Harriette's temperature went down to normal, but she stayed in bed for another fortnight before writing a desperate letter, twenty pages long, to the cruel Ponsonby:

> … Three weeks of bitter anguish of mind and body have changed, or rather matured, my nature so completely that even the expression of my features bears another character. My eyes are now open and I feel that, as the mistress of a married man, possessing an innocent, amiable young wife, I could no longer be esteemed or respected by the only being whose respect was dear to me. As lovers, then, Ponsonby, we have met for the last time on earth … I am a poor fallen wretch, who ask of your compassion one line or one word of consolation to save me from despair … I ask of God to soften your heart, that you may not torture me beyond my strength … I ask but to live for you, not with you …

Begging him to visit her once a year, with a chaperone, she concluded this ill-judged act of self-abasement with a plea that she might retain his friendship. She made the mistake so often committed by rejected women – she went on writing letters, desperately trying to keep dead embers alive. Ponsonby reacted as men usually do – he wrote her one brief, brutal note telling her she ought not to take things so seriously.

Harriette relied for comfort on her mother and her sister Fanny. The Duke of Argyll arrived from Scotland. Harriette had always liked him and would have found comfort in his company if he had not cruelly teased her about Ponsonby and 'that nasty sister of yours, Amy'. Amy was pursuing him. He had dined with Ponsonby the previous evening, he said, adding: 'I never saw him look better'.

Harriette could not bear it. She rushed towards the door, but Argyll took hold of her.

'It is all a joke, you credulous little fool,' he said heartlessly[3].

Panting for breath, Harriette replied: 'I can't run. Please, please, leave me. You torture me by staying. You may come back this evening.' He lingered, despite her obvious distress. As soon as Argyll had gone, she wrote a desperate last letter to Ponsonby:

> … You are quite happy, Argyll says; and I in the very flower of my age am dying. One line can relieve me perhaps from madness … I shall never write to you again … Adieu.

Answer came there none. Harriette sent Ponsonby's watch, chain and the ring he had given her to Amy. She could not bear to look at them. For six months she was really ill and suicidal. Harriette's anguish was genuine. Years later she wrote to Lord Byron:

> Lord, if only you could suffer for a single day the agony of mind I endured for more than two years after Ponsonby left me, because Mrs Fanny [Lady Ponsonby] would have it so, you would bless your stars and your good fortune … Heavens! how I have prayed for death, nights, days and months together, merely as a rest from suffering …

Harriette had learned a hard lesson and grown a carapace. Describing sexual passion as arbitrary and ungovernable, she armed herself against the temptation to fall romantically in love again.

As soon as she was able to speak, Harriette asked after her protegée in St George's Hospital. The girl was dying and Harriette arranged to have delicacies sent to her. The dying girl discharged herself and arrived in a cab, pleading to see Harriette, but the landlord would not let her in for fear of infection. Harriette's footman suggested she should be brought up by force, but the rest of the household were women and could not manage it. The poor creature stretched out her hands to Harriette, whispering: 'For the love of God, don't send me away from you, ma'am, in my last moments … '

'To the workhouse with her,' insisted the landlord. Harriette, far from well herself, travelled to the Marylebone workhouse with the girl, who died in her arms. This was a painful shock to Harriette, who was sick for a further week. The stories of the kindly old Jew and the ruined girl may be inventions rather than literally true, but indicate that Harriette felt kinship at this time with marginal members of society. She felt excluded.

Argyll returned to her side. His old mistress, Lady W—, was dying and Argyll was coming to terms with the prospect of losing her. He looked towards Harriette, but her hopeless passion for Ponsonby made her cool towards him and they remained just good friends.

Julia strikes a sour note, citing a letter from Argyll to Harriette after she asked him for £50:

> HARRY — Get your fifty pounds from those on whom you have conferred as many favours – you have never conferred anything on me for which the enclosure will not be to the amount of value received by
>
> > Your obedient servant …

He used red ink[4], and sent her a £5 note. However, Argyll brought Harriette news of the fashionable world.

'I have had a narrow escape!' said he.

'From what?'

'From rape!' said Argyll.

'Who, in this land of plenty,' said Harriette, 'is so very hard up?'

'Your sister Amy … '

Amy had asked him to see her to her carriage, offered him a lift and driven him without the option to her house, where she insisted he ate supper. He mocked her behind her back, but largely deserted Harriette to visit Amy on several occasions and indeed lived with her for a month and made her pregnant. Harriette says the shock of these painful events permanently damaged her own health.

Harriette had introduced the Duke to Amy, and had lent her clothes. Amy called and on seeing Harriette so ill, began blubbering. Harriette put it down to hypocrisy. She writes: 'and she intruded herself into my house, warm from the embraces of my lover, to show off tenderness!'

'You disgusting, deceitful creature!' cried Harriette, locking her sister into the room. 'Since you've forced your company on me, I'll make sure you regret it!'

She looked round for a weapon to strike her sister with, threatening to kill her.

Amy ran to the window and saw a boy in the street.

'Help me!' bawled Amy. 'There's a wicked woman up here, no better than she should be, has locked me in!'

'I shouldn't wonder,' said the boy, laughing and running away, 'a pair of you, no doubt.'

Harriette's temper had cooled and she was ashamed of her murderous impulse. She unlocked the door and told Amy to get out. Harriette convinced herself, and told Amy, that Amy was welcome to live with Argyll if she didn't object to Harriette's leavings. Argyll well knew, she said, that Harriette had been in love with Ponsonby for years.

Harriette later discovered that Argyll was worried about her health and that Amy's solicitude had been for effect.

Argyll's former mistress, Lady W—, died and he mourned her and let himself go, hardly bothering to shave. He called on Harriette, reminding her that when he had dearly loved her, she had not cared deeply for him.

'I'm unhappy now,' he said. 'I'm ready to devote myself to you, but I see small hopes of a steady return.'

'But then – you've been sleeping with my sister!' said Harriette. 'I find the idea disgusting. You have destroyed the possibility of our ever being more than friends for the rest of our lives. I only held back in my affection for you because you warned me, in a letter, that I had to share you with another woman. Are you being fair? I'm heart-whole now and intend to stay so for the rest of my life.'

They parted by shaking hands. Amy later gave birth to a son she named Campbell, but Argyll, despite arranging for straw to be laid in the street outside her door to deaden the noise of traffic[5], disclaimed responsibility and married soon afterwards.

Lord Craven's housekeeper, Mrs Butler, had been imprisoned at Newgate for debt. Harriette, deciding to palliate her own misery by doing good to others, went to visit her. Mrs Butler was surprised and delighted to see her. Harriette's first words to her were: 'I wish I could pay your debt.'

Mrs Butler was shocked to see how poorly Harriette was looking.

'What's happened to that merry, blooming face of yours?'

Harriette burst into tears, and handed her some money. Harriette sat with her an hour and promised to visit again. As she was leaving, she noticed a girl of about fourteen weeping bitterly, along with a sad elderly woman. Mrs Butler explained that the mother had seen better days. She had been paying 3s 6d (17.5p) a week for the hire of their bed, which was being carried away now they were penniless. Harriette gave them her last £1 note.

Next morning she was surprised by a visit from the Duke of Wellington[6].

He was as usual brusque but was shocked at her sad face.

'What the devil's the matter?'

'Something has affected me deeply,' said Harriette, tearfully, 'and I've been ill for more than two months.'

'Poor girl!' said Wellington. 'I was always afraid you'd get into some kind of trouble. Do you remember my telling you so? How much money do you want?'

He picked up a pen.

'I haven't any money, not a shilling, but that's not why I'm miserable.'

'Nonsense, nonsense,' said the bluff Duke, writing a cheque. 'Where the devil is Argyll? Why don't you make him pay your debts? I'll give you what I can afford now and if it's not enough you must write to me as usual at Thomas's Hotel. Good God! How thin you are! Were you sorry when I left you? You cried when I told you I was off abroad. I'm a cold sort of fellow. I daresay you think so, but there's no humbug about you, and when you cry I think you mean it.'

He stayed three hours and comforted her as best he could.

'His visit made no impression on me, except that I was grateful for his kindness in leaving me the money I wanted,' says Harriette.

She became asthmatic and settled in depression. Her affair with Ponsonby seemed in retrospect an unreal mockery, a broken dream. She was convinced she would die at once if she could only see him again. Her doctor feared consumption and recommended Italy. She trembled constantly.

She paid Mrs Butler a second visit, only to hear that the woman Harriette had given a pound to so she could keep her bed, had been telling the other debtors that Harriette was a 'mere kept mistress' with whom she would be ashamed to converse. Harriette was deeply wounded and indignant at such ingratitude from a person she had generously given her last shillings to. So much for sisterhood, she thought angrily.

Harriette defiantly began to recover. She called on her sister Sophia at eight in the evening. Soon Colonel William Fitzhardinge Berkeley[7], first cousin to Berkeley Craven, arrived. He was eldest son of Frederick Augustus, fifth earl of Berkeley, and Mary Cole, whom Lord Berkeley married in 1796. As he was born before his parents' marriage, William could not inherit his father's earldom in 1810. He appealed to the House of Lords, which repudiated his claim that his parents married in 1785. However, by cheating his younger brother Moreton into signing away his rights, William inherited a large fortune and was made Baron Segrave and Earl Fitzhardinge. He was a talented dancer and singer and a good conversationalist in French and English, but preferred low company, which led to his being shunned.

Berkeley Craven, early friend of Harriette, was a 'dangerous acquaintance' and William's next legitimate brother, Grantley F Berkeley, recalled that when Berkeley Craven and William Berkeley were together, the slang of the pugilist, the pickpocket and the highwayman and the vulgar term 'blowen' [whore] constantly marked their conversation, mixed with obscenities. A 'flash blowen' was what they coveted most and Colonel Berkeley gave the name to one of his favourite hunters. At the time of his death he was living with not one but two 'blowens' simultaneously. The diarist Greville wrote in 1835, 'The man is an arrant blackguard … for years acted on the Cheltenham stage … and is notorious for general worthlessness.' But he was generally lively and agreeable. Half an hour after Colonel Berkeley's arrival, in bounced Lord Deerhurst in an agony of tears.

'Oh Sophy! Sophy!' exclaimed his lordship, blubbering and wiping his eyes with a dirty red handkerchief. 'Oh, Sophy, I never thought you would have used me in this way!'

He accused her of infidelity with Colonel Berkeley and she denied it. Deerhurst rushed out of the room, like a barnstorming actor playing a tragic king, and sat on the stairs howling.

'What the devil's the matter?' said Colonel Berkeley.

Sophia's fat landlady told Lord Deerhurst not to take on so and gave him a glass of water.

'Could you have believed it, madam,' he asked her. 'Did you believe that this young creature was so depraved?'

Colonel Berkeley said he was astonished.

Harriette realized at once that it was a put-up job; Lord Deerhurst could claw back £200 a year on finding Sophia unfaithful to him. She told the men so. Deerhurst allowed Sophia £300, the extra £100 thanks to the intervention of Lord Alvanley.

'Nonsense!' said Colonel Berkeley, laughing, but nodding slily at Harriette. He offered not to call on Sophia again.

'My heartstrings are cracked!' roared Lord Deerhurst, darting out of the house. Berkeley had come with him, his own *vis-à-vis*[8] following. Berkeley and Harriette went in it to Lord Deerhurst's house in Half Moon Street. They were shown into his drawing room and waited for five minutes. Lord Deerhurst half-opened the door of his bedroom, which was next to it. He looked almost unrecognizably cheerful.

'Glad to see you both,' he said, wiping his hands with a filthy towel. 'Come in – excuse the disorder – only a bachelor's room, you know. I can't cry any more just now, because I've just washed my face.'

'Seriously,' said Berkeley, 'I want to know whether my attentions to Sophia are really disagreeable; I don't see how a man could command so many tears to flow at pleasure.'

'Oh, there was a boy at Westminster who could cry a great deal better than I can,' said Deerhurst.

'I won't believe you unless you sit down and produce real tears; but, first, ring for some proper wax candles, can't you? What are you doing with stinking tallow candles in your room?' asked Berkeley.

'Bachelor, you know, bachelor,' said Deerhurst, grinning.

'What the devil has that to do with it?'

Deerhurst ignored the question of candles, sank into an armchair and took out the dirty red handkerchief again. 'And yet,' said he, 'and yet, though I appear a wild, profligate, hardened young man, I never think of that sweet girl Sophia without its bringing tears to my eyes.' He blubbered aloud and the big tears rolled down his cheeks.

'This would melt a heart of stone,' said Harriette with irony, putting on her cloak. 'I'm off.'

'What! Don't you want any more?' said Deerhurst, jumping up and laughing.

'My brother Augustus is going mad for you,' Berkeley told Harriette, 'and you treat him very ill.'

'I shall have him locked up in a madhouse if he carries on behaving the way he did last Saturday – throwing himself on his knees in my box at the opera and acting like a tragic hero himself.'

'He's very handsome,' said Deerhurst.

'A mere ruffian!' said Harriette.

'Don't be so severe on poor Augustus,' said Berkeley. 'He's a sailor, you know, and upon my honour he is very fond of you. I want you and Sophia to favour me with your company to dine at Richmond on Monday, and, if you will trust yourself to my care, I will drive my barouche.'

'Willingly,' said Harriette.

'That's not all,' continued the Colonel. 'I am commissioned to intercede for Augustus.'

'I'm off, then,' said Harriette. 'Your brother's too rude for my present state of health. He'll soon tease me into a fever.'

'Upon my word,' said Berkeley, 'I can make him do just what I please. I've only put in a good word for him after I made him promise not to do or say anything that could possibly offend you.'

They agreed to meet on the following Monday.

'Let me come with you!' begged Deerhurst.

'No more of your rural fighting parties for me, thank you,' said Harriette. 'And I don't like eggs and bacon, nor do I care for a pot house to eat them in.'

To do him justice, Harriette admitted Lord Deerhurst had talents and could be very agreeable. He was not entirely selfish; he was devoted to his blind father, but he was to become increasingly unstable and eventually went crazy.

Harriette's favourite sister, Fanny, was being pursued by a Mr Napier, MP, of Hampshire, but Fanny did not like him.

'He was a long-backed youth with very fine eyes and that was all,' says Harriette, 'a sort of home-bred young man, not ungentlemanlike, but wanting tact and spirit.'

Fanny took Harriette out of the room in order to discuss Julia's plight. Julia had given up her romance with Cotton and fallen in love with Sir Harry Mildmay[9], who had loved and left her. In Julia's *Confessions* she takes great pains to distinguish herself from Harriette's way of life, accuses Harriette of scurrilous attacks on her, and implies that while her relationship with Cotton was deplorable and repented of, he was her only lover. She claims to have maintained herself and their six children on the interest on £4,000, which at the then usual rate of 4 per cent would amount to £160 a year, nothing like enough to manage a decent standard of living.

'I wish this Napier would attach himself to poor Julia,' said Fanny. 'Her children and her debts and her extravagance will send her to prison unless a rich man like him takes her under his protection. I don't fancy him myself, so I've left them together. This Napier, who has more than twenty thousand a year, can assist her and pay off all her debts, seeing that he lives on £3,000, and possesses in hard cash at his banker's more than £100,000.'

'Oh, the vile stingy monster!' said Harriette. 'Where did he spring from?'

'An Oxford college,' said Fanny, 'but his estates are in Ireland.'

When the sisters returned to the drawing room, Napier seemed to have fallen in love with Julia's manner and to be delighted with her conversation. However, he soon placed himself by Fanny's side, to plead his cause with her as usual. Harriette declared her intention of leaving and Fanny said she would go too. Napier called her a coquette and a false deceiver.

'You promised to let me see you home,' he complained.

'Can't help that,' said Fanny, kissing her hand to him and hurrying downstairs. He handed them to their carriage.

'Go back and talk to Julia,' said Fanny.

Harriette added that Julia was a niece of Lord Carysfort and daughter of the Honourable Mrs Storer, lady in waiting, 'and the most graceful creature breathing'.

Napier went back and – 'I'll tell you what happened some other time,' says Harriette discreetly.

Fanny was not prosperous herself; her allowance from the late Mr Woodcock's estate was paid irregularly and she owed money to her son George's tutor. Harriette offered to pay Fanny's debt and to maintain the boy herself during the holidays.

'My mind was now a complete blank,' she writes. 'My imagination was exhausted; my castle had fallen to the ground and I never expected to rebuild it … my cool judgement told me that Ponsonbys were not often to be met with. I had no fancy for going downhill, so I bought a great many books … I lived very retired, and when I did go out or admit company it was more because I was teased into it than from any pleasure I found in society.'

She does not explain how she paid her rent now Ponsonby no longer took care of her. Her housekeeper was instructed to keep creditors at bay by telling lies about her mistress's mad violence, requiring 'at least three people to hold her'. She flirted with Julia's faithless love, Sir Harry Mildmay, who declared, as men often do, that he could not stand scenes, reproaches or hysterics. He called on Harriette and, she says, 'proceeded, in a very summary way, to practical lovemaking', which she rejected as Julia's friend. Her loyalty to Julia, though, had its limits.

Notes to Chapter Five

1. Page 56: Ponsonby (1770–1855) does not seem to have been a kind husband and Lady Ponsonby was not hoodwinked. Since he was married, the relationship with Harriette was furtive; even Julia was unaware of it. Harriette says her affair with Ponsonby lasted three years; implicitly from 1806, when his father died, to about 1809, but it seems to have gone on longer or started earlier, and almost certainly overlapped other relationships. Harriette shuffles her stories like a pack of cards. On 30 December 1812 – the year of Sophia Dubochet's marriage, when Harriette was living with Lord Worcester and also involved with the Duke of Leinster – Lady Granville Leveson-Gower wrote to Lady Georgiana Morpeth:

> Lady Ponsonby is beautiful beyond description, and an engaging, affectionate, gentle person, with an understanding crushed by his affected contempt and brutality, for I am convinced he is in fact desperately in love with her all the time. They have, I hear, come to an understanding ... He is to give up Miss Wilson and all that sort of thing, ... Lord Ponsonby is very affected and agreeable, for his affectation is not offensive ...

Lord Ponsonby never did give up 'all that sort of thing'. Sir John Ponsonby, writing the family history a century later, does not mention Harriette, but says that Ponsonby had 'serious love intrigues with Lady Conyngham and Princess de Lieven, but did not allow his love affairs to interfere ... with his duties as an ambassador' (*The Ponsonby Family*, p80). Princess de Lieven was the wife of a Russian diplomat who in 1811 was appointed ambassador to London.

2. Page 58: Bleeding 'to let out bad humours' was a cure-all until the twentieth century. As late as the 1940s, Miss Mabel Wood, in the Forest of Dean, asked the doctor to bleed her. Slapping Miss Wood on the shoulder, he replied: 'My dear little woman, you need all the blood you can get.'

3. Page 58: Aristocratic males knew how to close ranks and keep uppity courtesans in their place. Parallels can be found in the 1960s, with the Cliveden set. Lady W— remains unidentified. One commentator says Argyll's mistress was a daughter of the Earl of Jersey, but this more probably refers to Lady Paget, formerly Lady Caroline Villiers, who married Argyll as her second husband, after her divorce.

4. Page 60: *Confessions*, p19. Julia presumably saw Argyll's letter. She cannot have seen the correspondence between Wellington and Harriette in the 1820s because the triple alliance had been broken by Fanny's death and Harriette's removal to Paris. The story of Wellington's non-existent red ink probably begins here (see Appendix).

5. Page 60: Straw was laid outside the homes of invalids to protect them from traffic noise. 'In the straw' was a euphemism for childbirth.

6. Page 61: Like other events in Harriette's *Memoirs*, this account is either invented or transposed in time; in 1810 or 1811, when Sophia was in her early teens, Wellington was abroad, fighting the Peninsular War. Harriette makes him return from that campaign on leave; in fact, he went in 1809 and did not return for five years. Without mentioning dates, Harriette implies that the Duke's military successes were all behind him when they met. He did not become a duke till 1814, having previously risen from being Sir Arthur Wellesley to baron to viscount to earl to marquis, but Harriette, who always preferred to use later titles, calls him Wellington throughout and in this instance I have followed her.

7. Page 62: Colonel William FitzHardinge Berkeley (1786–1857). A detailed account of his career can be found in *My Life and Recollections* by his legitimate younger brother the Honourable Grantley F Berkeley (vol 1, 35–48 and *passim*). Berkeley was a member of the smart Four-in-hand Club, 'one of the glories of the days of the Regent': 'The symmetry of the horses, the arrangement of the harness, the plain but well-appointed carriage … ' resembled in their perfection of detail 'a choice work of art' (Gronow, *Reminiscences*, p274).

In 1823 Colonel Berkeley and another brother acted in an amateur production of Shakespeare's *King John*, when he took the part of the Bastard Falconbridge, which caused eyebrows to be raised. Mrs Charles Arbuthnot said he was a bad actor (*Diary*, 19 August 1823). He was not really a Colonel and was known for a while as Lord Dursley, but, according to Julia, Harriette cheerfully called him 'Bastard'.

8. Page 63: A *vis-à-vis* was a light carriage with two seats facing each other.

9. Page 64: Sir Henry St John Mildmay, fourth baronet (1787–1848), MP for the city of Winchester, in 1809 married Charlotte Bouverie, who died the following year. In 1814 he married her sister, the divorced wife of the fourth Earl of Rosebery. In Harriette's novel *Paris Lions and London Tigers* he appears as 'Sir Violet Sigh-Away'. See also Chapter 12.

6

Fred Attempts Rape

Little George Woodcock, Harriette's troublesome nephew, came to her next morning. Before the week was out he had broken open Harriette's jewel box, stolen her money, kissed the housemaid and fought the footman, for young George was an enthusiastic boxer. Harriette looked forward to returning him to Leytonstone, where he and Julia's three boys had boarded with an elderly Frenchman for the past four years; no educational provision was made for her girls.

Colonel Berkeley and his brother Augustus arrived to take Harriette and Sophia down to Richmond as fast as four high-bred horses could carry them. Flashy Colonel Berkeley ordered a dinner as ostentatiously extravagant as Deerhurst's had been stingy. He suggested half an hour in a rowing boat while it was being cooked. Harriette had come a long way since the days, a decade or so previously, when she had given herself to the carroty lad who plied in his boat for hire. Now she was with Colonel Berkeley, who astonished the boatmen by tipping them a five-pound note[1]. She was pleased to discover that Colonel Berkeley could talk. Harriette adds that conversation was not considered a necessary accomplishment in gentlemen of her day. She comments shrewdly:

> A man is a gentleman, according to Berkeley Craven's definition of the word, who has no visible means of gaining his livelihood; others have called Lord Deerhurst and Lord Barrymore and Lord Stair gentlemen because they are lords; and the system at White's Club, the members of which are all choice gentlemen of course, is and ever has been never to blackball any man who ties a good knot in his handkerchief [cravat], keeps his hands out of his breeches pocket, and says nothing … I like a man who can talk and contribute to the amusement of whatever society he may be placed in.

They discussed Shakespeare. Augustus fancied himself in the role of Romeo. Colonel Berkeley saw himself in the role of Douglas[2], a brave soldier. He pressed his suit with Sophia and complained that if she meant to refuse to live with him, she ought not to have encouraged him. Sophia, all modest blushes, gently hinted that everything depended on his intentions; what settlement was he meaning to make on her?

Colonel Berkeley was enraged. He blustered that he didn't have to buy any woman's reluctant embraces. Why should he give money for a cold-blooded creature 'who calculates at fifteen years of age what the prostitution of her person ought to sell for?' He turned nasty because young Sophia knew her own market value and was holding out for fair treatment; he bullied the child till she shed tears.

Sophia, who was seduced at thirteen by Lord Deerhurst

Harriette told him she and her sister had been insulted and wished to leave: 'Will you procure us some safe conveyance? No matter what.'

Colonel Berkeley apologized and offered to take them home. The journey took place in silence and the Colonel avoided Sophia afterwards. Such were the hazards of the lives the sisters led.

Next day Harriette drove her wilful nephew George Woodcock back to school in Leytonstone and warned him that if he were to be expelled she would see to it that he was sent away to sea[3].

Another sister, whom Harriette identifies merely as Paragon, was respectably married, with two sons and two daughters under seven. Their mother educated them at home, influenced by the theories of Jean-Jacques Rousseau[4]. Her plan was to keep them innocent; she believed that nurses and servants could teach them only bad grammar and worse morals. They must never hear about thieves, murderers, or deceit. Nothing was to be considered indecent that was natural, and they were to take laxative pills every night.

Pretty Paragon's husband was out when Harriette called, but she was surrounded by her lovely children.

Little Mary chattered of love; she knew everybody fell in love and she was in love herself.

'With whom?' asked her mother.

'With my brother John, of course, mamma. When can we get married? I can't wait much longer.'

'To bed, to bed!' said Paragon. 'You must all go to bed directly.'

'Already?' said Harriette. 'It isn't six o'clock yet.'

'Never mind,' said Paragon, fanning herself. 'I'm tired to death of them. And they're always asleep before seven.'

In five minutes, four naked children were laughing, romping and playing with each other. Sophia, not yet two, toddled after her brother Henry, who was nearly four.

'Little Sophia, bred in the school of nature, handled her brother rather oddly, I thought,' writes Harriette demurely.

'All nature's own sweet work!' said their mother dreamily.

'Mamma! Mamma!' called Henry.

'What's the matter, my love?' said Paragon.

'Is Sophy to have my diddle to keep?'

'No, my love,' answered mamma with calm dignity, 'not to keep – only to play with.'

Harriette was more anxious for Julia's 'poor dear beautiful children' than for her own nephews and nieces; she called on Julia and urged her to provide for them by means of Mr Napier. When was he coming next?

'The odious long-backed creature will call here tomorrow,' admitted Julia, pulling a face in disgust.

Harriette, pitying her, offered to write to Julia's uncle, Lord Carysfort.

'Don't mention that unfeeling wretch!' cried Julia. She was convinced that money left to her had been misappropriated. She had twice written to her uncle, but her second letter had brought only a crushing reply:

The person from whom you expected a legacy showed a becoming horror and disgust at your vile profligate conduct by withdrawing your name from his will.

Julia, usually so reserved, sobbed aloud.

We get a glimpse of Julia's virtuous cousins at about this time in a private letter from Sarah, Lady Lyttelton to her brother, the Honourable Robert Spencer:

I have been to two soirées – not assemblies, but whist parties – at Lady Carysfort's … There were but very few steady people there, and one card table, where Papa risked his shillings, while Mama and Lady Carysfort, I and her daughters, sat amusing ourselves as we could … I delight in those girls; they are so thoroughly right and respectable, and, besides, have such warm, good hearts, and good educations, and their conversation is just what pleases me … They are not very pretty, and rather cold to strangers – that is, entirely without coquetterie [*sic*] or vanity – so that I dare say they will remain the 'Lady Probys' for ever[5].

Lady Lyttelton's judgement was shrewd; plain girls with good principles may please their mothers and their mothers' friends, but are rarely pursued by men; only one of Lord Carysfort's daughters, Lady Elizabeth, found a husband, marrying a Mr Wells in 1816. Did these staid virgins, trapped in their dull social rounds, secretly envy their wicked cousin Julia the moment of romantic folly which had precipitated her exuberant and uncontrolled fertility, and a life of adventure?

'Never mind them,' said Harriette. 'Napier's your man.'

'But his vanity makes me sick,' said Julia. 'He doesn't just want my body; he wants me to prove that I love him – and that's physically impossible.'

Harriette, remembering Fred Lamb's demands, fell silent.

'What's become of Amy and Argyll?' Harriette asked, after a pause.

'Amy's very proud of Argyll and also of her pregnancy, and lives in hopes that her unborn babe by the Scottish laws may yet be the Duke of Argyll.'

'She's bespoken a boy, then?'

'She lives in hopes.'

Harriette felt a pang: 'Is he as tender and loving to her as ever?'

'I've heard nothing to the contrary,' shrugged Julia.

Harriette persuaded herself she was not jealous, merely sickened.

Julia returned to the pressing problem of Napier, long-backed and short-legged: 'If I were to consent to his wishes and he didn't provide for my children, I'd drown myself in the Serpentine,' she wailed. Harriette told her she ought not to have brought so many children into the world, but now they existed Julia must provide for them. She promised to meet Julia in their opera box that evening. Berkeley Craven and the Duc de Berri joined them and so did the Duke of Leinster, who for lack of a chair was forced to stand. Harriette despised this Irish peer[6], still only nineteen, handsome, stupid and – according to her usual gibe – stingy. However, she admits he was honourable and paid his bills. He retained his Irish accent, despite four years at Eton, and had a tiresome habit of agreeing with everything people said, all smiles and sweet good humour.

'I knew I should find my big cousin the Duke here,' said handsome Harry De Roos[7], poking his curly head into the box.

'Come in, pretty Harry,' cooed Harriette.

The boy blushed. 'I'm so melancholy,' he said, sighing.

Leinster explained that Harry's mother, Lady De Roos[8], was sending her son to a private tutor next day. The boy was frightened by Leinster's tales of being miserable when boarded out in a family called Smith. Invited by Harriette to share these memories, Leinster said he had shared with two other lads.

'We got up at six and cleaned our own boots. Breakfast was thick slices of bread with just a little salt butter. After that we had three large books placed in front of us and we had to read for five hours, taking notes. Dinner was a roast joint one day, hash the next. and mince the day after that. The meal was enlivened by the three Miss Smiths.'

'What sort of animals were they?' asked Julia, laughing.

'Miss Jemima wore a sort of false rump, sticking out like this,' said Leinster, sticking out his own behind.

'Was she pretty?' asked Harriette.

'Too much like a dead horse,' said Leinster.

'Gorgons all three, and all over thirty, I'll bet,' said De Roos gloomily, with a groan.

'But you're not going to live with Mr Smith,' said Julia, sensibly.

'That's true,' said De Roos, brightening. 'There can't be anywhere else like it, can there, cleaning boots and the Miss Smiths and everything?'

'No,' said Harriette, 'you must hope for the best. Being without the Miss Smiths will be something, at any rate.'

'Thank God I've done with private tutors!' said Leinster.

'How do you like Oxford?' asked Julia.

'Delighted with it,' replied the Duke, adding that Brummell no longer counted at Christ Church[9].

'Who do you think sets the fashion there now?'

'Yourself, perhaps?'

'No. Nothing is asked but whether Harriette Wilson approves of this or that! Harriette likes white waistcoats – Harriette praises silk stockings, et cetera. I asked my friend, the young Marquis of Worcester, why he didn't curl his straight hair. Do you know what he said? "Harriette considers straight hair the most gentlemanlike." When I asked him if he knew Harriette, the Marquis admitted he had never seen her, adding: "I ran up three times to the opera, on purpose; but she didn't make her appearance. Will you present me to her?" I refused him; I'm the only young man at Oxford who does know you,' said Leinster proudly.

The Marquis of Worcester was no ordinary Oxford undergraduate, even in

The Marquis of Worcester walking in Hyde Park

the early nineteenth century, when the university was a playground reserved for the well-born. He was, at eighteen, already one of the dandies and, as a regular visitor to Oatlands, country estate of the Duke and Duchess of York, was in the same circle as Lord Craven, Lord Yarmouth, Lord Alvanley and Beau Brummell. There were no women's colleges in those days, though Oxford and Cambridge were well supplied with prostitutes to service the young men. But Worcester, later a member of the Four-in-hand Club, aspired to the heights of fashion, had heard of Harriette and decided he wanted a piece of the action. He intended to have the most celebrated mistress in London. His parents, the Duke and Duchess of Beaufort[10], were religious people, low church evangelicals who avoided the theatre as a haunt of immorality. Their son was ready to spread his wings.

'Is he good-looking?' asked Fanny.

'Not at all,' said Leinster.

Meanwhile, Napier came into the box, the other gentlemen having left, and monopolised Julia. Young Lambton, second son of Lady Ann Wyndham, was about to proposition Harriette when Lord Kinnaird entered and whispered in her ear, in French: 'Mademoiselle Harriette, you mustn't corrupt him.'

Lambton reddened and looked uncomfortable.

'What's the matter?' asked Julia.

'I understood what Lord Kinnaird said, and I think he was very rude. I'm twenty-one and I have no intention of being treated like a child.'

'Then you're old enough not to take offence where none was intended,' said Harriette briskly. 'Lord Kinnaird knows you only by sight.'

'He had no reason to take such a liberty,' returned the young man, who huffed and puffed and sulked.

Harriette refused to let the young Duke of Leinster see her home. She found two letters on her dressing table. She recognized the familiar round script of her nephew George Woodcock. Knowing he would not write unless he wanted money or clothes, whips or cricket bats, and happening at that time to be poor, she did not open George's letter at once. Her other letter was addressed in an unfamiliar hand, which she suspected was disguised. Inside was a bank note [draft] for £200, in a blank cover. Harriette decided Providence must be taking care of her, for she now, at twenty-five, had no regular protector, though Fred Lamb would not leave her alone. The mysterious donor she decided must be Ponsonby, a thought which gave her more pain than pleasure, because she wished to think of him as heartless and unworthy of her affection.

George's letter read:

'MY DEAR AUNT, – I hope you are well, as this leaves me at present. Excuse this bad writing as I am so very bad, and my head aches fit to split, but I am ordered this very moment, before the post goes out, to acquaint you with my accident, as Monsieur Codroie says, perhaps, you may wish me to come to town, to have the rest of my teeth put to rights, the fact is then, to be short, dear Aunt, I was running just now, and I hit my face against another boy's head, and broke out my two front teeth,

Your affectionate Niece [*sic*]
GEORGE WOODCOCK

Fred Lamb turned up late one night at Harriette's house and talked for an hour of Argyll, of Ponsonby, and the past when he himself had shared a bed with Harriette. Then he impatiently seized her hand and roughly kissed her. She wore no stays and her dress tore as he grabbed at her beautiful breasts, of which she was so proud. Harriette was still obsessed with Ponsonby, and had a backlog of resentment against Fred. She fought back. Fred's pride was outraged. He had lived with this woman; how dared she refuse him when he fancied a bit of fun? What was the matter with her? What was she being so fussy about? She had to be taught a lesson. Fred thrust a hand between her legs, rousing her not to desire but to fury. He attempted to push her down on the sofa, but she tugged at his hair, pulling a swathe of it out by the roots. She scratched and bit.

'You little vixen!' he growled. 'I'll kill you if you hurt me again.'

He grabbed her by the throat and almost choked her. She thought she was going to die. She panicked and kicked him hard on the shins, which brought him back to his senses. Panting and dishevelled, he relaxed his grip. A strong man, he could easily have strangled her. Never for the rest of her life did she forget that moment, and never did she forgive Fred Lamb. Terrified, she rushed upstairs and double-locked her door. Fred went about telling the story of how he had attempted to rape her, but she was 'so in love with John Ponsonby that she was cruel even to me last night! I tried force too; but she resisted like a little tiger and pulled my hair!'

Harriette reflected that he had acted as though he had a right over her person, a right to persecute her with brutal force and lay murderous hold of her throat, because she was not his humble slave.

'In fact, I was a good deal afraid of Fred Lamb at that time, and could not but feel provoked at the idea of a young man going about the world, always laughing, and showing off the character of a fine, good-tempered, open-hearted, easy, generous … fellow. … He is now an ambassador, and just as well off as ambassadors usually are; yet, in my present poverty, I have vainly attempted to get a hundred pounds out of him,' she wrote bitterly in the *Memoirs*.

Next morning Harriette woke late and asked for a cup of chocolate, then very much a rich person's beverage. Before she could drink it, the Duke of Leinster arrived and Harriette went down in dressing-gown and slippers.

'I've brought little George some strings to mend his fiddle with and, if you'll give it me, I'll string it for him,' said His Grace.

Harriette rang for George's fiddle and Leinster set happily to work, chattering the while.

'My brother, Fitzgerald, is involved with a woman. He told me she was a Venus. Last night I wanted to go home and think of you, but Fitzgerald literally dragged me to Number 2, Upper Norton Street. We were shown into a parlour by an old dirty duenna, who regretted that her mistress was engaged.

'"Good gracious!" I said. "Fitz, you aren't going to wait?"

'"Yes," said my brother mysteriously. "Do please be quiet. I shall ruin her if I'm found here. The man who keeps her is a captain in the horse marines."

'"For heaven's sake, let me be off!"

'But Fitzgerald forced me to stay there for half an hour. I was frankly terrified of being caught there by the horse marine, hidden on his premises after two o'clock in the morning. The much-dreaded horse marine, instead of going out by the street door as we expected, strutted into the parlour in search of his hat. Not that he looked like a horse marine to me – looked more like a city tradesman. Nevertheless, I made myself as small as possible and tried to hide behind the skimpy curtain. Fitzgerald thought all was lost, so he became bold from desperation. He folded his arms and stared at his rival, who started back and looked frightened, stammering that he had only brought the lady home safely from the opera, no disrespect intended.

'Fitzgerald, being quick-witted, grasped the situation at once, and assumed the character of the fictitious horse marine. Waving his hand with much pomp towards the door, he fixed his back against the fireplace and said, "No offence, my good fellow, no offence! Only there's the door, you know, and unless you prefer making your exit by the window, never let me see your rascally ugly face in this house again." The poor wretch crept out trembling and we burst out laughing. The frail fair one came in and my brother bowed and said, "Madam, since I have been allowed to make such a valuable acquaintance as that of your horse marine[11], my conscience won't permit me to interfere with his happiness."'

'Now, Duke, there's the door,' said Harriette, in imitation of Fitzgerald, laughing. Leinster left at two o'clock that afternoon.

Harriette's sister Amy had been expecting to marry Argyll. Late in her pregnancy, Argyll broke the news to her that he was going to marry Lady Paget, a divorcee. Amy cursed robustly and had hysterics. The baby did not arrive by the expected date and Argyll accused her of fooling him with a phantom pregnancy. When her labour pains began, Amy screamed at the doctor, 'Give me a pair of scissors – I'm going to cut my throat!'

'My dear lady,' said the doctor, 'I should be happy to oblige you, if it weren't putting my own neck at risk.' He turned to the nurse, warming his hands by the fire. 'I always let them holler and make as much noise as they like. Meanwhile, as I shall have to stay the night here, I'll thank you for some warm blankets on that sofa, with a cup of tea and a bottle of wine.'

Amy gave birth to a son and Argyll travelled northwards for his wedding to Lady Paget[12], which took place in 1810, Amy having been abandoned. Amy told everybody he had killed her, but recovered and consoled herself by saying the new Duchess, who already had eight children, was too old for Argyll, her second husband; Lady Caroline Elizabeth Villiers had married Lord (Henry William) Paget who was a member of Crockford's gambling club, along with Count Palmella, Prince Esterhazy, and later the young Disraeli and Bulwer-Lytton. Lord Paget had run away with the Lady Charlotte Wellesley, wife of Sir Henry Wellesley and sister-in-law of the Duke of Wellington. Wellesley was awarded damages against Lord Paget of £24,000. Divorces followed; it was suspected that they were arranged by agreement among the parties – then an illegal proceeding – and remarriages took place.

Lady Paget had at one time had an affair with the Prince of Wales. She was a beauty and sister to Lady Ponsonby. It was a world in which everybody knew everybody else, and pairs of brothers married pairs of sisters. Relations between Wellington and Paget were strained after Paget stole Wellington's brother's wife, but Wellington could not do without Paget's soldiership for ever. Lord Paget (later Lord Uxbridge) commanded the cavalry at Waterloo in 1815 and was created Marquis of Anglesey. He is famous for saying during the battle: 'By God, I've lost my leg,' to which Wellington replied, 'By God, sir, so you have'.

One day the Duke of Leinster, his cousin Harry De Roos and Sophia were about to sit down to dinner with Harriette when Lord Deerhurst was announced.

'Dear me, how tiresome,' said Sophia.

'Please don't send him in here,' chorused the two young men.

Harriette went down to ask him what he wanted and told him whom she was entertaining.

'Oh, I do so want to know the Duke of Leinster: please introduce me,' pleaded Deerhurst.

'No,' said Harriette. 'I shall do no such thing. That's frank and flat. If you don't like Sophia's dining here, you can take her away, that is, if she'll agree to go with you, but I'll never present you to any friend of mine. Sophia told you this morning she was going to meet the Duke of Leinster and his cousin.'

'Oh, I don't mind in the least,' said Deerhurst. 'Only please be a dear, good creature and present me to the Duke of Leinster.'

'In every way, you are the meanest man on earth,' sighed Harriette.

'You refuse me, then?'

'I do, and you must allow me to wish you good day, as we're going to dinner immediately.'

'I must introduce myself then,' said Deerhurst, brushing her aside. He ran into the drawing room, where Harriette's guests were waiting, swept off his hat with a low bow and said, 'Duke, allow me to introduce, and earnestly recommend to your notice, Viscount Deerhurst.'

Leinster was not a proud man, but he did not care to be intruded upon. He bowed very slightly in silence, with a frigid half-smile. Harry De Roos was both proud and shy, so took no notice except rising from his chair to acknowledge Deerhurst's greeting.

Deerhurst was too crass to be abashed by two mere boys and seated himself near Sophia, who always agreed with the latest person to speak.

'Well, Sophy my love, are you glad to see me?'

'Very glad indeed,' said Sophia.

Harriette could bear it no longer. 'Let me tell you something, Lord

Deerhurst,' she said. 'I don't like quarrelling and especially not in my own house; but seriously, these gentlemen were expecting to meet just me and Sophia and your intrusion is the other side of enough, as the saying is.'

'It really is the other side of enough,' echoed Sophia.

'If His Grace will say he wants to get rid of me, then I'm off,' said the incorrigble Deerhurst and the well-bred young Duke politely pressed him to stay. Deerhurst was not stupid and could even be amusing. Tired of being snubbed by so many respectable people, he set about winning Leinster's friendship and succeeded. Deerhurst talked of boats and sailing, praising such Irish nobility as lived on their estates[13].

Henry Luttrell called after dinner to say that Amy was giving her first party after her confinement and to offer an invitation. During Amy's liaison with Argyll relations between her and Harriette had cooled, but Harriette asked Leinster and De Roos if they would like to take her to Amy's with them.

'Most willingly,' they said.

'Make no apologies for not asking me,' said Deerhurst. 'I haven't the courage to face that tartar of a sister of yours without a special invitation.'

Harriette took her revenge by inviting Luttrell to inspect the jewels Deerhurst had given Sophia. In smart jewel boxes were a necklace of large green glass beads and assorted junk. Everybody laughed, Deerhurst loudest of all.

'And then,' he spluttered, 'having won the young lady by dint of these valuable jewels, and an annuity agreement not worth sixpence, I invite the company to congratulate me.'

Luttrell stared at Deerhurst in disgust; Sophia agreed it was amusing indeed; the others were embarrassed.

'Lord Deerhurst,' said Harriette, 'Sophia is my sister, and if she chooses to be insulted and ill-treated by you, it shan't be in my house, where you weren't invited.'

Sophia burst into tears: she didn't want to be insulted and would rather not go back to Lord Deerhurst, a nasty man (she said) who hardly washed.

'Why don't you live with Harriette?' said Deerhurst.

Harriette was sickened. 'The man's not worth crying over,' she said to Sophia. 'You're welcome to live with me. In the meantime, let's drive to Amy's.' Deerhurst whispered in Sophia's ear that Harriette was jealous and wanted him for herself.

Sophia agreed. 'I think Harriette is a little jealous,' she said, 'so I'll go home with you, to make her mad.' And off they went.

Amy's drawing room was full. She seemed less fierce than before the birth. She was still handsome, but her Siddonian features were softening. Like her younger sisters, she had rich, abundant hair; hers was jet black. She wore a yellow satin dress, fastened below the breast with a gold band, and she glittered with jewels. Amy was outshone though by her younger sister, Fanny, Harriette's favourite. Fanny was wearing a pale pink crepe dress which set off her bright auburn curls and dark blue eyes. Her arms were bare except for bracelets clasped with a single brilliant ruby. She had a lovely smile; her figure was slim and elegant. Julia was like her, except that her hair was darker and her teeth uneven. They were often taken for sisters. Both were dressed in the height of fashion. Julia wore a frock of silver lamé and a Turkish turban of bright blue, fringed with gold. Both were remarkably graceful, the best dancers in the room. Harriette habitually wore white gauze over white satin, with dangling earrings of diamonds, rubies or turquoise; white was the most fashionable colour, because expensive to maintain.

It was on that same evening that Harriette first saw Colonel Parker. He was not good-looking, but was under thirty, comfortably off and wanted to take Fanny as his mistress. Harriette advised against it; if Colonel Parker wanted Fanny, why didn't he marry her?

'She shall bear my name, and I will show her all the respect a wife can require, and she shall always find me a gentleman,' said he. The Dubochet sisters, well-dressed as they were, had to make do with what they could get. Glittering appearances masked debts and a terrifying insecurity.

Notes to Chapter Six

1. Page 68: Five pounds plus board and lodging was a lower servant's annual wage.

2. Page 68: Archibald Douglas, fourth Earl of Douglas (*c* 1369–1424), fought on Hotspur's side at the Battle of Shrewsbury. Falstaff in Shakespeare's *1 Henry IV*. ii.4, fights him and pretends to be dead.

3. Page 70: As, according to Julia, George Woodcock came to a bad end, he presumably misbehaved at school. She tells us that he became a midshipman, was turned out of the navy for theft and became a pirate. He died in a fight (*Confessions*, p342).

4. Page 70: Jean-Jacques Rousseau (1712–1778), who believed in the 'noble savage' and taught that civilisation was inferior to nature.

5. Page 71: 22 February 1811.

6. Page 72: Augustus Frederick Fitzgerald, third Duke of Leinster (1791–1874), was a godson of the Prince of Wales, and educated at Eton 1806–10. He married in 1818 Charlotte Augusta, daughter of the Earl of Harrington, and spent most of his life on his Irish estates.

7. Page 72: Gronow lists young De Roos with Argyll, Alvanley and Worcester as one of 'the dandies of society (*Reminiscences*, p44)'. De Roos, like Fred Lamb, Brummell, Wellington, Leinster and Gronow himself, was an Etonian. He was the son of Lord Henry Fitzgerald.

8. Page 72: She assumed the name De Roos in 1806, after the title 'Baron de Roos' had been in abeyance for more than a century.

9. Page 72: Oxford's smartest college, founded by Cardinal Wolsey, and familiarly known as 'The House.'

10. Page 73: Henry Somerset, Marquis of Worcester (1792–1854) was aristocratic indeed. The Beaufort dynasty is descended from John of Gaunt and is one of England's noblest families. Worcester's father was the sixth Duke, Lord Lieutenant of the counties of Monmouth, Brecknock and Gloucester, Lord High Steward of Bristol, Warden of the Forest of Dean. Worcester's mother the Duchess was previously Lady Charlotte Sophia Leveson-Gower, daughter of the first Marquis of Stafford and sister of Lord Granville Leveson-Gower.

11. Page 76: Chambers's *Dictionary* gives 'horse marine' as 'a person quite out of his element; a member of an imaginary corps'.

12. Page 76: Lady Jerningham spoke for many when she wrote to her daughter Lady Bedingfield:

> It is a very odd affair and Lord Paget will not admire meeting with his Quondam Wife with the higher Rank of Duchess and an obsequious Husband, for he has always treated her with the most shameful Contempt … it is in fact a most irregular proceeding (13 November 1810).

Jane Austen wrote to her niece Fanny Knight: 'What can be expected from a Paget, born and brought up in the centre of conjugal infidelity and divorces … I abhor all the race of Pagets' (13 March 1817).

Lord Glenbervie's *Journal* (30 June 1818) describes the Pagets as 'a family so remarkable for … personal charms but domestic depravity sometimes bordering on incest of many individuals of the present race and of both sexes … '

Ten years after the marriage, Harriet, Countess Granville saw the Duke and Duchess of Argyll walking in Hyde Park, and observed to her sister that they looked 'fat and lazy' (letter to Lady Georgiana Morpeth, 6 October 1820).

13. Page 78: Irish landlords who lived on their rents in England, neglecting the people on their estates, were criticised by those with social consciences. Maria Edgeworth's didactic novel, *The Absentee* (1814) is directed at this evil. Her hero, Lord Clonbrony, returns to Ireland to take up his responsibilities.

7

MISS HIGGINS'S PECCADILLOES

Amy had a friend who called herself Lucy Armstrong, mistress of Colonel Thomas Armstrong – noted wit, member of Crockford's Club and aide-de-camp of the Duke of York. Lucy was a neat little person who embroidered her own gowns. Lucy and the Colonel, after seven years together, had several children and, although Lucy was a good manager, funds were short. The colonel decided, at the age of fifty, that they must prevent any more babies.

'We'll be good friends, my love,' he told Lucy, who was some twenty years younger than he was, 'but only friends, from now on.'

Lucy found this ultimatum dismal news.

'We can't have separate beds, my dear,' she protested, 'because there isn't a spare bed in the house.'

'True, my darling,' returned her dear Tommy, 'but I'm afraid that friends is all we can afford to be, now and in the future.'

The prospect of living for ever with the man she adored without the comfort of physical satisfaction appalled poor Lucy, who burst into tears.

The Colonel was sympathetic but adamant. He patted her kindly on the shoulder, while she pined for passionate embraces.

'Go and see your friend Amy, my dear,' he said. 'It'll cheer you up. And now there won't be any more babies, there's no need for you to slave at making my shirts! I'll be able to afford to have them made up by a seamstress now.'

This was small consolation to Lucy, who was proud of her skilful needlework and enjoyed doing it. Lucy thought of all the attractive men who frequented Amy's salon, and was afraid she might succumb. She was pursued by many, but gently repelled all advances, and kept her hunger to herself. She was cruelly snubbed by George Brummell, who said to her, 'Would you like to dance?'

She rose, curtseyed politely, and said: 'I'm never tired of dancing.'

Instead of leading her on to the dance floor, he fixed his eyes for a few seconds on her face and said quietly: 'You have a dancing face.' Then he walked away.

Lucy was doubly humiliated; her partner refused to make love to her and the most fashionable man in London refused to dance with her, after arousing her expectations. She felt cheated.

Leinster was still in Harriette's orbit. Harriette was amazed that anybody could have such good looks 'without a mind'. He agreed with whatever anybody said. He was all smiles and sweet good humour, and 'not the first fool I have met with, who required wit and talent in a mistress'.

Harriette was hungry for fresh romance.

'Life to me isn't worth living without a bit of love,' she complained. 'Who do you think the best worth having, Duke?'

'I think the Duchess of Beaufort's brother, Lord Granville Leveson-Gower[1], the handsomest man I ever saw,' replied Leinster.

'How does one get to see him?'

'Can't help you – and if I could, I wouldn't,' was the ungracious reply.

Harriette persuaded herself that Ponsonby – who was indeed a cold fish – had trifled with her feelings and taken advantage of her youth and inexperience, an astonishing judgement. Following her usual practice, she wrote to Lord Granville, requesting him to come and meet her in Regent's Park at eleven o'clock on a Sunday morning, yet demanding that – despite her boldness – he must treat her with deference.

He replied:

I do not usually answer such letters; but there is something so eccentric and uncommon in yours, that I cannot resist complying with your request, therefore you will find me at the appointed time and place.

G L GOWER

As the time drew near, it struck Harriette that she had no idea what the man looked like. How was she to distinguish him from any other handsome man out for a walk? She dressed in her best clothes, and turned up on time. A tall gentleman was looking about him. Harriette decided he was no good as a love-object and hoped for better luck, but there was nobody else about who looked at all like a lord.

'This must be Leinster's Apollo,' she thought; and it was. Lord Granville had in 1804 been appointed ambassador to Russia. He was now in his late thirties, Harriet still in her mid-twenties. She walked him up Primrose Hill, then on towards Hampstead – then a small village – and eventually back to Great Portland Street, a distance of some five or six miles. At last he came to a stop and pulled off his hat to wipe the sweat off his face.

'I can't go any further,' he gasped. 'I'm not used to walking, and this sunshine is so very oppressive! Please permit me to accompany you to your house, if only to sit down and rest, or I shall collapse and die!'

'I'm really sorry,' said shameless Harriette. 'I hope our pleasant walk in the country will have no such fatal consequences. But I'm afraid you're not the man I'm looking for.'

Lord Granville smiled and bowed and said good morning. He said he was

Harriette walks Lord Granville Leveson-Gower off his feet

greatly amused by such eccentricity. Perhaps he congratulated himself on a lucky escape; his mother had written to him when he was twenty-one telling him he was attractive, and warning him against 'artful women'. For many years he had been the lover of Lady Caroline Lamb's mother, Lady Bessborough, giving her two children, but in 1809 he had married Lady Bessborough's niece, Harriet Cavendish, daughter of William, fifth Duke of Devonshire who, after her husband was created first Earl Granville, became Harriet, Countess Granville. Lady Granville's voluminous correspondence survives as a valuable source of information about her times.

Harriette Wilson, seeing that her pick-up did not lead to passion as it had done with Lorne, decided that love, like money (?!), came when one was not thinking about it. She had been sentimentally in love with Lord Byron for years and wrote to him introducing herself[2]. Nothing came of it and she says she was without an emotional centre to her life.

Fanny was happier. 'It's all settled,' Fanny said. 'I'm to be Mrs Parker.'

'I hope you'll be happy,' said Harriette wistfully, 'but I wish you were married.'

'Why should poor Parker marry a woman with a ready-made family?' said Fanny, and Harriette thought it best to hold her tongue. Fanny and Parker planned a honeymoon in Brighton and were then going to Portsmouth, where his regiment was stationed. Harriette suggested that she and Julia should join them, taking a house in Brighton together. This was arranged.

A Miss Eliza Higgins called to apply for the post of paid companion to Harriette, the vacancy having been created by the departure of Miss Hawkes, who had married a cousin. Miss Higgins looked forty and admitted to twenty-six. Her clothes were out of date, her skin was bad and she was heavily made up. She had small twinkling eyes. She said her previous employer had been the Countess Palmella, wife of Amy's admirer, the Portuguese ambassador, in South Audley Street: 'I have been educating her children.'

In reply to Harriette's question, she said that had been her first situation.

'What were you doing before that, pray, ma'am?'

'Why,' said Miss Higgins affectedly, 'you see I was daily – nay, hourly! – expecting to get settled in life. I had a small property and I went to Bath. Several of my friends had found charming husbands in Bath. However, time slipped away, madam, and by some strange fatality or other I exhausted my little resources, and didn't manage to get settled in life; and that's the truth of it.'

Because of the tenuous connection with Amy, Harriette engaged her.

At a dinner party given by a rich former tradesman called Quinton Dick, Amy was escorted by Lord Yarmouth, a member of the Prince's inner circle. He was known punningly as 'Red Herrings' because of Yarmouth's fishing industry and his red hair. Fanny was escorted by Lord Alvanley, and Lucy Armstrong by the Honourable John Ward, who was bawling puns in Latin and – as always – laughing at his own jokes. Luttrell and Nugent were, as usual, together. Harriette asked Lord Alvanley why he had left his regiment.

'I was afraid of getting shot,' replied Alvanley, in his usual quiet way.

'Weren't you just as afraid of being called a coward?'

'I was in two engagements and distinguished myself in both. I don't mean to say I ever volunteered anything, you know, but I never ran away. They didn't reward me for my services as I expected. I'm content to have retired on half-pay. I shouldn't have gone into the Guards at all if I'd known they were going to leave London.'

Offered Madeira, Alvanley asked for champagne instead: 'I can get Madeira at home.'

Julia had been persuaded to come, despite her dislike of Amy, who had been making up to Sir Harry Mildmay simply because Julia adored him. He had dropped Amy, but that did not prevent her teasing Julia about him and reducing Julia to tears.

After the ladies withdrew, Julia announced that Sophia had moved in with her; Deerhurst had only succeeded in making Sophia feel neglected.

'Why didn't you bring her with you?' asked Amy.

'In the first place,' said Julia, 'I've promised your mother that Sophia shan't go out except with my own children; and in the second, she was not invited.'

Sophia's virtue was gone, but appearances had to be kept up.

Lucy Armstrong said to Amy, 'Oh, Amy, my Tommy was so good and kind last night.'

'How do you mean?'

'Guess,' said Lucy coyly.

'Very well, I do; but I can't calculate the brave colonel's — er — forces.'

'Oh. Only once,' admitted Lucy.

The gentlemen joined them. Alvanley, twiddling a stick, managed to break one of his host's mirrors. Mr Dick grew sulky and said, with a bow, 'Since the honour of your lordship's company is so expensive, I really must decline it in future.'

'I'm really very sorry,' replied Alvanley. 'Of course, I couldn't insult you by buying you another.'

'I assure you,' said the irritated Mr Dick, 'I'm not touchy.'

'I wouldn't dream of imposing on you by doing anything half so rude,' blandly returned the lordly dandy.

After tea and coffee, they all went to the King's Theatre, but before Lord Yarmouth parted from them, he invited the women to dinner. They said they had no time, as they were going to Brighton.

'Name your own day,' said Yarmouth. 'Come tomorrow if you like; but come you must.' Harriette had met him when she lived in Brighton. He 'had long been our family's friend, equally at hand to congratulate us on our marriages, our simple fornications, our birthdays or our expected deaths,' she writes.

'Tomorrow then,' said Amy quickly, without consulting her sisters or Julia.

'What a fine thing it is to be an elder sister,' said Harriette, causing Amy's notorious bad temper to explode. Lord Yarmouth politely offered to send a carriage for his guests the next evening.

At the theatre Harriette found the Duke of Leinster in her box. He seemed agitated.

'I'm glad you have no men with you,' he said. 'The friend I mentioned has come all the way from Oxford[3] on purpose to try to get introduced. He has to go back to college tonight and I must confess that I don't want him to be disappointed.'

'What nonsense!' said Julia. 'And who is it, pray?'

'The Marquis of Worcester,' replied Leinster.

'Is he handsome?' asked Harriette.

'Not at all.'

'What's he like?' asked Fanny.

'Not like anybody much, except perhaps his father,' said Leinster. 'He's a long thin, pale fellow, with straight hair.'

'Don't worry,' said Harriette. 'I shan't meet your friend if I can help it. I always tell everybody I know not to bring men without asking my permission first.'

'I know you do; Lord Worcester has had the same answer from several of your friends he has applied to. There he is!' said Leinster, leaning over towards the stalls. 'There – do you see a very tall young fellow in silk stockings, looking steadfastly up at this box? You know, upon my honour, he won't wear trousers or curl his hair, because he heard that you dislike it.'

'Very flattering,' said Harriette. The Three Graces stared at the young man through their opera glasses, embarrassing him. Harriette decided he would not do for her any more than his maternal uncle, Lord Granville Leveson-Gower, had done. Within five minutes, she had forgotten his existence. She was unaware that he was a close friend of Lord Alvanley, Lord Yarmouth, Lord Craven and George Brummell.

Lord Frederick Bentinck came and asked when Harriette would go with him to the pleasure gardens at Vauxhall.

'We shall never get to Brighton at this rate,' said Fanny dolefully. 'I'm so looking forward to some donkey-riding. It looks as though Harriette is going to keep us in town all summer again, like she did last year.'

'Summer!' cried Brummell, entering in a furred greatcoat. 'You don't mistake this for summer, do you? A little more of your summer will just about finish me.' He pulled up his fur collar.

'Upon my honour, I think it's very hot,' said Leinster. 'It has to be hot, doesn't it? After all, it is August.'

'I can never tell the difference,' said Fred Bentinck impatiently. 'I only feel cold when I put on a greatcoat. But then I've always so much to do, and that's what keeps me warm. Once and for all, madam, are you coming to Vauxhall on Monday night? If you are, I'll put off my sister and accompany you.'

Harriette said yes, despite protests from Fanny and Julia, as Fred Bentinck always amused her.

'Remember Monday,' he said as he left the box to make room for Mr Napier and Colonel Parker, followed by Lord William Russell, son of the Duke of Bedford. Lord William asked pathetically what there was about him to recommend himself to her notice: 'I'm a poor little wretch without fortune or wit.'

Harriette comforted him by telling him he was good-looking, high-born and high-bred. She wanted to encourage the most 'humble, little gentlemanlike being' she ever met. Lord William was of course a younger son, so had no inheritance. Like the Duke of Argyll, Lord William was a frequent guest at royal dinner parties; he became British Ambassador at St Petersburg. On 6 May 1840 he was murdered by his Swiss valet, Courvoisier, who stabbed his master in bed and was hanged on 6 July the same year. Lord William's wife, Lady Charlotte Villiers, was the sister of Lady Ponsonby and the Duchess of Argyll.

As Parker and Napier left the box, Lord Deerhurst came and Lord William, afraid of intruding, went. Lord Deerhurst said: 'I don't often introduce gentlemen to ladies, and perhaps I'm taking a liberty now; yet I hope you can have no objection to my making you known to the Marquis of Worcester.'

Harriette bowed coldly, because she had often asked Deerhurst not to bring people to her without permission. However, the young Marquis blushed so deeply, and looked so humble, that it was impossible for her to treat him otherwise than politely. Convinced she would never love him, she engaged in small talk with Deerhurst, who at his best could be lively and pleasant. The Marquis scarcely spoke, but Harriette observed that his manners were perfect.

Leinster was bored and cross that Deerhurst had achieved what he could not, though he tried to hide it. Harriette offered to take Lord Worcester to Amy's; Worcester seemed confused.

'Do come, my lord,' said Fanny, who liked what she had seen of him. He politely refused.

'Nonsense,' said the hearty Deerhurst. 'What a fellow you are! I really can't make you out. I give you my word that less than an hour ago he declared he'd give half his lifetime to sit near you and talk to you for an hour, and now you invite him to spend the evening with you, and he seems frightened to death.'

'You men are all wicked, cruel deceivers,' said Harriette lightly.

Worcester blushed and protested that he had reasons for not going to Amy's, but Harriette must not imagine for a moment that he was indifferent to her.

Deerhurst put out a hand and touched Harriette's head, saying it was as pretty as a race-horse's.

'I've never seen such beautiful hair,' said Worcester timidly.

'Put your fingers into it,' said Deerhurst. 'Harriette doesn't mind how you tumble her hair about.'

Worcester refused to do anything so familiar.

'Oh no,' responded Harriette. 'Anybody may pull my hair about. I'm no prude; I like it.' The information that she was not a prude was surely superfluous.

Worcester, trembling, lightly touched her hair and Harriette suspected that he was madly, wildly, romantically in love with her.

'Come with me,' said Deerhurst to Leinster, and they left.

'May I,' said Lord Worcester eagerly, 'may I, when I come back to town, venture to pay my respects?'

'Certainly,' she said, 'if I'm in town, but we're going to Brighton.'

She told him her health was delicate. Just before the curtain dropped, Worcester explained shyly that his reason for not visiting Amy was that Lord Deerhurst had told him she was unkind to Harriette. Harriette thanked him, but warned Worcester that she was not in love with him.

'My love-days are over,' she said. They said goodnight, as he had to return to Oxford. The Three Graces went to Amy's, with Colonel Parker, who showed Fanny every respectful consideration; they seemed very attached to each other. Leinster was still miffed. Harriette found this tiresome and told him so. She left early and Leinster took her home.

Next day Harriette and her paid companion walked in Hyde Park.

'How do you do? How do you do?' said Lord Fife[4], Major General in the Spanish army and a great lady-killer. His mistress was La Mercandotti, the Spanish ballerina who had become the rage of London at the age of fifteen.

'Who's your frriend?' he asked, giving Miss Higgins a look suggestive of intense admiration. 'Aren't I going to be introduced to your frriend?' He retained a strong Scottish accent.

Harriette did so and he talked to Miss Higgins as though she were irresistible, suddenly interrupting himself to comment: 'What a funny little bonnet you've got on!'

After he left them, Miss Higgins was in raptures. 'Charming man, ma'am, the Earl of Fife! Now that's a man a poor weak female would find very hard to resist. His lordship is so condescending, so polite!' That evening she was so overcome by his compliments that she was incapable of helping Harriette to dress. Harriette's footman[5] brought a note from Lord Fife himself, asking to be allowed to spend the evening with Harriette and her 'lovely companion'. She did not show the note to Miss Higgins, but sent a message: 'My compliments only; tell his lordship I'm very sorry, but I can't write, because I am this instant getting into my carriage to dine with Lord Yarmouth,' and followed her servant downstairs.

Lord Yarmouth had invited no men to meet the ladies, but kept them entertained with good food, good wine and brilliant conversation. He had more general knowledge, writes Harriette, than anybody she ever knew. His politics chimed with hers, as his whole family were Tory. He seemed on top of every subject imaginable, from drawing to horses; painting to cock-fighting; rhyming, cooking and fencing; religions of every creed; languages ancient and modern; claret or burgundy; champagne or bad port; furniture, venison, or the breeding of parrots. Lord Yarmouth showed his guests miniatures – all of good-looking women – coins, medals, watches, snuffboxes, drawings and portraits from his distinguished collection.

'No such thing as foisting sham Vandykes or copies from Rubens' on him,' writes Harriette admiringly. He left his artworks to his secretary – actually his illegitimate son – Sir Richard Wallace, and they were eventually bequeathed to the nation as the Wallace Collection, now housed in Manchester Square, London. Yarmouth's mother, the second Marchioness of Hertford, was mistress of the Prince Regent, and Yarmouth was at this time a royal favourite. He indulged every appetite and the diarist Greville described him as 'an example of undisguised debauchery'[6]. Harriette says he talked of commissioning Sir Thomas Lawrence[7] to paint her with Amy and Fanny, but no such picture exists.

Though the tea and coffee, like the meal, were excellent, Yarmouth made a good-natured complaint to his servant about the cream.

'Really,' said Yarmouth to his visitors, 'for a man who keeps a cow, it's a shame to be served with such bad cream.'

'I never knew you kept a cow,' said Harriette. 'Where is she?'

'In Hyde Park, just opposite my windows'[8].

He showed the guests a small detached building, consisting of a luxurious dressing room, small sitting room and a bedroom with erotic pictures on classical themes. This apartment opened on to Park Lane. Lord Yarmouth drew to the attention of the ladies the convenience of entertaining female visitors in secret after the servants had gone to bed, having prepared a delicious supper.

'I find it advantageous to be discreet,' he said slily. 'Nothing could induce me to mention the name of any woman who has favoured me. In the first place, I like variety and I want to succeed with the next one, and in the second, it's dishonourable. I know a young woman of family who had an intrigue with a young dragoon. I found out quite by accident and refused to keep it a secret until she had made me as happy as she had made him.' He chuckled.

'Was that honourable?' asked Harriette drily.

'Perhaps not,' replied Yarmouth, 'but I couldn't help it, now could I?'

The party did not break up till two o'clock, when they all returned home in Lord Yarmouth's own carriage.

Next morning brought a note from Lord Fife, wishing to drink tea with Harriette and her 'charming friend'. Harriette was tickled to think she was playing second fiddle to Miss Eliza Higgins for the amusement of the Earl of Fife. She wrote on the back of his note:

Going to Vauxhall; but you may come tomorrow at nine.

Miss Higgins nearly fainted when she heard the Earl of Fife was coming.

'Oh dear, ma'am, what would you advise me to wear? If it's not a liberty, could you lend me the pattern of your sweet blue cap; I'll sit up all night to make one just like it —'

'All this energy about drinking tea with a rake of a Scotsman you know perfectly well wouldn't marry an angel? And you pretend to be virtuous?'

'Certainly,' said Miss Eliza Higgins, reddening.

'Fiddlestick!' said Harriette.

Miss Higgins burst into tears.

'Lord Fife wants to make your acquaintance and I would never stand in the way of a woman's chance to better herself; so – guessing from all the raptures you have expressed about this womaniser's attachment that Countess Palmella's former governess is no better than she should be – I agreed to receive his lordship. But since your tears of virtuous indignation have convinced me I did you an injustice, I'd hate to bring him together with a virgin.'

Harriette sat down to write a refusal.

Miss Higgins was breathless with agitation. 'Surely you're not putting off the Earl of Fife?' she gasped.

'I think it wrong to introduce such a loose man to an innocent woman.'

Miss Higgins begged and pleaded in vain.

'Well, then,' said Miss Higgins, 'I confess that I just once —'

'Once what?'

'I had a slip — er — yes, a slip!' Miss Higgins's handkerchief was at her eyes.

'What do you mean by a slip? Are we talking about a petticoat or an intrigue?'

Miss Higgins said she preferred to talk of a slip because it conveyed a less definite idea of loose morals. Harriette wrote the refusal to the Earl of Fife.

'If yours was only an accidental slip, we can surely recover your reputation?' Harriette's hand was extended to ring the bell.

'Oh dear! Oh dear!' cried Miss Higgins. 'What poor weak creatures we are! I'd quite forgotten the General –'

'General who?'

'Why, General – but you'll keep the secret?'

'Silent as the grave, of course.'

'Have you ever heard of General Mackenzie?' Miss Higgins spread her hand across her forehead.

'You mean Fred Lamb's General in Yorkshire?'

'The same, madam, a fascinating man!'

'True,' said Harriette. 'I remember all the servant girls and dairymaids in Yorkshire found him irresistible.'

'How true!' said Miss Higgins, with a deep sigh.

'So you've forgotten the Earl of Fife already?'

'Oh, his lordship is quite another thing.'

'And another thing is what you wish for?' said Harriette.

'Oh indeed, ma'am, you are too severe! These little accidents do happen. I know several women who have made excellent wives after a slip or two; they only serve to fortify our virtue.'

Harriette picked up her pen. 'Well then,' she said, 'in case the wicked Lord Fife should break through the formidable bulwark of virtue that has been fortified already by two intrigues, I shall positively send a refusal.'

Miss Higgins grew eloquent; who knew what might turn up?

Julia had had a miscarriage, but hoped to be able to come to Brighton. She sent for Harriette, who found Fanny and Sophia – looking prettier and happier now she had left Lord Deerhurst – at Julia's bedside. Fanny had moved to Hertford Street, Mayfair, and called herself Mrs Parker, but had called to see Julia.

'My dear Fanny,' said Harriette, 'what am I to do with your boy George? We shall never make a scholar of him and he doesn't want to be a sailor.'

'Flog him! Flog him!' said Amy. 'I flog my boy Campbell all the time.' As Campbell was not yet two, this seemed to Harriette excessive.

About that time a Russian gentleman was introduced to Harriette. She asked him if he knew Benckendorff.

He laughed. 'Oh, yes! Benckendorff is my particular friend. He wanted to come to England with me; but, he said, he'd made such a fool of himself about some woman here, Amy I think he called her, that he was ashamed to show his face within a thousand miles of her or her friends.'

Harriette, always at war with Amy, passed this news on to her sister, whom she found in bed with the Honourable Arthur Upton[9].

'Benckendorff's the fox and I'm the grapes,' said Amy. 'No doubt he's heard I'm Mrs Sydenham.'

'Alias Upton,' said Harriette unkindly.

Notes to chapter Seven

1. Page 83: Leveson-Gower is pronounced as 'Loosen-Gore'. Harriette made a mistake in his Christian name; he was not Lord George, as she calls him, but Lord Granville Leveson-Gower, later first Earl Granville (1773–1846), third son of the first Marquis of Stafford. Elizabeth, Lady Holland met him in Florence when he was twenty-one and described him in her *Journal* (29 January 1794) as 'remarkably handsome and winning'. Lord Granville once lost £20,000 at a sitting to William Crockford, who proceeded to set up a gambling club (Gronow, *Reminiscences*, p255). In 1823 the Duke of Wellington accidentally 'peppered Lord Granville's face with nine shot, fortunately he missed his eyes but it has given him a great deal of pain. Those *battues* [shooting parties] are dangerous things,' wrote the Countess Cowper to her younger brother Fred Lamb (16 January 1823).

2. Page 85: Any letters Byron may have written to Harriette have disappeared, but hers to him were found among the Byron papers.

3. Page 86: Oxford to London was a day's journey.

4. Page 89: James Duff, fourth Earl of Fife (1776–1857). He was made a Lord-in-Waiting to George IV, but was dismissed for voting against the malt tax.

5. Page 89: Harriette does not tell us who at this time was paying her rent or how she was able to employ servants. The gap between Ponsonby's departure and full protection from her next lover may well have been shorter than she admits.

6. Page 90: Francis Charles Seymour-Conway, Lord ('Red Herrings') Yarmouth (1777–1842) became third Marquis of Hertford in 1822. Lord Yarmouth was a great epicure and considerably annoyed Lord and Lady Holland in 1812 by luring away their French chef, Morel.

Harriet, Countess Granville wrote to Georgiana, by then Lady Carlisle, about him (20 January 1832): 'Such powers of being delightful and captivating, *grands manières*, talents of all kinds … all spent in small base coin.'

Lord Yarmouth owed his advancement to the fact that his mother, Lady Hertford, was until 1820 mistress to the Prince of Wales, and in 1812 he was appointed Vice Chamberlain of the Prince's household. He was married in 1798 to an illegitimate daughter of the fifth Duke of Queensberry. As Lord Hertford, he is the original of Lord Monmouth in Disraeli's *Coningsby* (1844) and of the wicked Lord Steyne in Thackeray's *Vanity Fair* (1847). One suspects that behind Thackeray's Becky Sharp lurks the ghost of Harriette Wilson's *Memoirs*, bowdlerized for a prudish Victorian readership. Harriette writes kindly of Lord Yarmouth, but he was notorious for drunkenness and sexual excess. Greville described him after his death as:

Between sixty and seventy years old, broken with various infirmities from a paralysis of the tongue, he has been in the habit of travelling about with a company of prostitutes who formed his principal society, and by whom he was surrounded up to the moment of his death, generally picking them up from the dregs of that class, and changing them according to his fancy and caprice. Here he was to be seen driving about the town and lifted by two footmen from his carriage into the brothel, and he never seems to have thought it necessary to throw the slightest veil over the habits he pursued ... [He] posted with his seraglio down to Richmond. No room was ready, no fire lit; nevertheless he chose to dine there amidst damp and cold, drank a quantity of champagne, came back chilled and exhausted, took to his bed, grew gradually worse and in ten days he died (*Diary*, 10 March 1842).

7. Page 90: Sir Thomas Lawrence, RA (1769–1830).

8. Page 90: Cows grazed in St James's Park as well as Hyde Park.

9. Page 92: Later General Sir Arthur Upton, who told Gronow he was present at the dinner when the Prince of Wales took his revenge on Brummell for 'Who's your fat friend?' by saying 'I think we had better order Mr Brummell's carriage before he gets drunk.' (*Reminiscences*, p51) After the restoration of the Bourbons, Upton was among the élite of Parisian society.

8

A Trip to Brighton

While Harriette was dressing for Vauxhall in her usual white on white with diamond earrings, Miss Higgins wondered aloud whether the Earl of Fife would be there. Vauxhall and Ranelagh Gardens were popular resorts for respectable families, aristocrats and prostitutes.

Lord Frederick Bentinck arrived before Harriette was ready.

'You always keep me waiting,' he said. 'Quite a bore. I can't amuse myself in this room, because I daren't open any of your books. I'm always afraid of hitting on something indecent or immoral.'

'Come,' said Harriette. 'We shall be late if you stand prosing there.'

'I'm thinking,' said Fred Bentinck, not moving.

Harriette took his hand and pulled him towards the door.

'You can think as we go along.'

'Stop a minute and listen. I take a big risk, going out with a woman like you.'

'What do you mean by a woman like me?'

'Well — a woman — a woman, to be blunt, of your loose morals!'

'You blockhead,' said Harriette, running downstairs.

The gardens were crowded, and Harriette attracted admiring glances, so that Lord Frederick grew proud of having her on his arm and pressed forward into the throng. She tugged on his arm until they reached the deserted walks.

'What are you afraid of?' said Lord Frederick.

'Not of your loose morals,' said Harriette, taking her revenge. 'But I'm used to going about with with the chosen Apollos of the age and I shall get terribly laughed at if I'm seen at Vauxhall with an ugly-mug like you.'

Frederick Bentinck laughed cheerfully. Harriette says it was all good-humoured teasing; perhaps it was. Bentinck told Julia he could listen to Harriette's conversation for a year at a time. Harriette returned home at four o'clock. Miss Higgins[1] was still up stitching the cap which was intended to fascinate the 'Thane of Fife'. Her first question was whether he had been in the gardens.

Next evening after dinner the ladies sat at the teatable waiting for Lord Fife, who was invited for nine o'clock. Miss Higgins's new cap would have suited her if she had not been haggard from staying up late. Her soft fine hair was loose, a style too young for her. She looked constantly at her old-fashioned

French watch. Harriette, playing the unaccustomed role of second fiddle, dressed casually. The clock struck nine.

'Is his lordship punctual generally speaking, pray ma'am?'

'Quite the reverse, I believe,' said Harriette, half-asleep.

'You have a good heart, I know, ma'am, and we females ought to assist each other in all our little peccadilloes,' said Miss Higgins.

'Well?'

'I'm going to ask your advice, since you know his lordship's tastes better than I do. Should I be netting a purse, or would it have a better effect to put on my gloves and be doing nothing?'

The footman came in with a letter sealed with a large coronet, saying a servant waited below for an answer.

'I'll ring when it's ready, James,' said Harriette.

'It's an excuse from the Earl of Fife!' said Miss Higgins, white under her face powder. It was in fact from the Earl of Sligo, whom Harriette had met the previous day for the first time, asking humbly to 'pass this evening alone with you'.

Harriette was enraged. She seems to have inherited her father's touchiness. A woman known to be a kept mistress, who wrote to strangers and then picked them up in the street, was surely making an unnecessary fuss about Sligo's overture, particularly as she was in the habit of accepting £50 notes in lieu of formal introductions. Violently she rang the bell, scaring Miss Higgins.

'Who's waiting?' she demanded.

'A servant in livery,' replied James.

'Send him up to me.'

A stylish and well-mannered servant in a cocked hat entered the room, with many bows.

Harriette handed him the opened letter with a flourish. Icily she said, 'There's some mistake. This letter can't be for me, as his lordship was presented to me only yesterday. Take it back, young man, and say from me that I request he'll be careful how he misdirects his letters in future; this one must have been an accident, no doubt caused by his writing after dinner.'

The man bowed low and took the letter with him.

'The Earl may still arrive, then?' hoped Miss Higgins.

In another minute, in walked the Earl of Fife, in a black and tan broad striped satin waistcoat with a gold watch and chain with several seals. As agreed in advance, Miss Higgins played the role of modest maiden, overdoing it to the extent of saying only 'Yes' or 'No, my lord' with downcast eyes. Once she briefly mentioned her dear grandmamma and grandpapa. Harriette, looking at her companion's long, plain face, brilliant with agitation and pearl powder, thought the Earl of Fife must be blind. However, he was genuinely attracted, called Miss Higgins an amiable creature, and placed a valuable ring on her finger. He did not leave till after midnight, having obtained permission to write to her.

Harriette congratulated Miss Higgins on her success. 'This has done more than your six seasons at Bath, and brought a noble earl to your feet. We'll now say goodbye. Make any use you please of your conquest, and accept my thanks for being so truly ridiculous.'

Miss Higgins bridled, muttered something about female jealousy, and said she was leaving anyway.

'Agreed, then,' said Harriette, holding out her hand. 'I promise never to say anything but good of you to Lord Fife ——at least not before he's tired of you.'

Miss Higgins took the hand. 'Goodnight,' she said, leaving the room. She came back.

'You'll forward any letters that may arrive from the Earl of Fife?' she asked.

'Certainly.'

'In that case, I propose going to my grandmamma's tomorrow.'

And so they parted.

About a fortnight later Harriette set off for Brighton. Leinster begged her before she left to say she liked him more than Worcester. Harriette had forgotten all about Worcester. Lord Fred Bentinck rode by the side of her carriage for the first ten miles.

'I hope you'll soon come back. As you know, I don't make speeches or pretend to be in love with you. You're a loose woman, and you know I hate anything immoral. But I'm sorry you're leaving. Pray do conduct yourself with some degree of propriety at Brighton; and take care of your health. I've written to my friend Dr Bankhead about you.'

A good house on Marine Parade had been hired. Amy had a new admirer, Boultby, who lounged on the sofa, and the sentimentality of this relationship got on Harriette's nerves. Soon it got on Amy's as well.

'Get up,' she said, rudely pushing him off the sofa.

'No,' said Boultby. 'Not until I've had another kiss.'

He took it.

'For heaven's sake, get up,' snapped Amy. 'I came down to Brighton for the fresh air and for three days I haven't breathed any. I'm sick of you.'

He hoped she was joking, but she threw him out and afterwards always refused to admit him.

Lord Robert Manners, a soldier, third son of the fourth Duke of Rutland, was very attentive to Harriette and taught her to ride[2]. At the Colonel's invitation, he took her in to dinner at the officers' mess at Lewes. He spoke little but once got the better of George Brummell.

'Those leathers aren't bad; who made them?' asked Brummell.

'Why, the breeches-maker,' said Bob Manners, speaking very low. Brummell for once was silenced by this retort.

Lord Yarmouth, later third Marquis of Hertford, nicknamed 'Red Herrings' because of his red hair, and with a pun on the fishing industry. He was cultivated, but debauched

Lord Yarmouth was a constant visitor. One evening he escaped from a royal party at the Pavilion and arrived with a hamper of claret, saying he couldn't stand the old women at Brighton. Julia and Sophia wrote to say they had changed their minds and would be staying in London. Dr Bankhead left his card. Harriette avoided him, as he had a reputation for taking advantage of female patients, but a return of her old chest trouble decided her to call him. He breezed into her bedroom as if he were an established friend.

'What's the matter, my sweet young lady?'

Harriette could barely speak.

'Fever? Yes. Oppression? ah! Cough? Hey? Do not speak, my sweet creature. Do not speak. You have been exposing that sweet bosom –'

He put his giant hand on her breast and attempted to seduce her.

'I am indeed a terrible fellow —'

Harriette pushed his hand away.

'Dr Bankhead, I really must —'

'Be quiet, my sweet! Quietness is everything in these inflammatory fevers. Hush! Lie very still —'

'This is an unmanly advantage —'

'Take me altogether, as much or as little as you like, sweet —'

'Dr Bankhead, I must ring the bell —'

Managing to reach it, she tugged on the bellrope till her maid appeared.

'Show Dr Bankhead out and whatever you do, don't leave him alone with me.'

'Good morning, my sweet, comical lady!' said Dr Bankhead as he left the house.

After a couple of months, Amy and Harriette were both tired of Brighton. The Duke of Leinster joined Harriette in London and was followed by the young Marquis of Worcester, who sat with her for two hours talking about Byron's poetry, music and riding until interrupted by Leinster. Worcester's friends assured Harriette he was crazy about her, but she found it hard to believe, because he treated her with such deferential courtesy, with no mention of love or sex. Leinster, convinced that Worcester was a successful rival, talked of going to Spain, where Wellington was fighting the Peninsular War against Napoleon.

'Lord Worcester never makes love to me!' Harriette told Leinster. 'This morning he didn't even offer to shake hands, and when I held mine out he seemed to shake and tremble.'

'When are you seeing him again?' sulked Leinster.

'I have no idea: all Lord Worcester said was that he'd like to call sometimes to pay his respects.'

Harriette next called on Fanny, and found Lord Alvanley and Amy with her. Fanny's long-term admirer, Baron Tuille, told them that Worcester kept asking people whether Leinster had left for Spain.

'That's a very fine young man, that Marquis of Worcester,' said Amy. 'I should like to be introduced to him, only I suppose Harriette, with her usual jealousy, will prevent me.'

'On the contrary,' said Harriette, 'Fanny heard me invite him to your party after the opera, the very evening he was presented to me, and he refused to go.'

'I've some news for you,' said Fanny. 'Sophia has made a new conquest! An elderly gentleman in a curricle, with a coronet. He does nothing from morning till night but drive up and down before Julia's door. Julia is cross and says it looks so very odd.'

'Talk of the devil,' said Alvanley, as Julia and Sophia came into the room.

Teased about him, Sophia described her admirer as 'a very dowdy, dry-looking man'.

'But then, his curricle!' said Harriette. A carriage with a coronet on it was something. Sophia said a ride in it would be nice. Julia grumbled it was a nuisance.

'So it is, abominable; I hate him, and his curricle too,' agreed Sophia.

Baron Tuille said Worcester was desperately jealous of the Duke of Leinster.

Harriette pooh-poohed the idea that Worcester was in love with her.

'Depend on it, he's in a bad way,' lisped Lord Alvanley.

As Harriette's cab drew up to her door, Worcester was riding past.

'I'm going to Astley's with the Duke of Leinster,' said Harriette cheerfully. 'Would you like to come too?'

'If you really want me to,' said Lord Worcester, reddening.

'Oh, I shan't break my heart if you don't,' said Harriette.

'I don't want to be intrusive,' said Worcester, 'but I'm most anxious to say a word to you before you go to Astley's tonight.'

'Leinster is coming for me at half-past seven,' said Harriette, 'so call at seven.'

The young man, all effusive gratitude, rode off. Harriette went upstairs, where she was surprised to find the Duke of Leinster sitting in her drawing room at her pianoforte.

'I have a favour to ask,' said Leinster. His usual boyish smile was gone; he looked pale and interesting.

'My dear little Harry,' he said, passing a hand across his curly head. 'I'm bothered to death by Worcester's perseverance. I'm going to Spain. I can't ask anything from you as a right, but I implore you not to receive Worcester as a visitor till I've gone, I hope in less than six weeks. I'd be gone sooner, but there are things to arrange to do with my coming of age[3].'

Harriette was touched by his sincerity. She kissed away a tear. 'Don't go, Leinster,' she said. 'I'll tell Worcester I shan't see him as long as you're here.'

The boy's face brightened.

'When?'

'Lord Worcester is coming here at seven and I'll give him his marching orders.'

Leinster hurried off, cheerfulness restored, intending to be back in time to take Harriette to Astley's circus.

Harriette was eating her dinner at the then fashionable hour of six (whatever Lord Alvanley thought) when Worcester arrived.

'If you will allow me,' he said with his usual formal politeness, 'I propose to accompany you to Astley's.' He hesitated. 'But you must realise that it's very hard on me to see the Duke of Leinster, or indeed anybody else, take you home.'

'I realise no such thing,' retorted Harriette. 'You're not my husband or even my lover, and you've never mentioned love to me. I hope you aren't in love with me, because —'

'Because what?' said Lord Worcester, breathlessly.

'Because my old friend, the Duke of Leinster, is very much irritated by your visits, and —'

'But you told me you didn't care for him!' said Worcester.

'I said I wasn't in love with him, and I'm not, but I don't like teasing him. So to be blunt – and one has to be blunt when one is in such a hurry – I've promised to ask you, as a favour, not to come here any more.'

The boy blushed scarlet, then went deadly pale. Indignantly he picked up his hat, then put it down in despair. Harriette felt sorry for him and held out her hand.

'Listen, my friend,' she said. 'I can't quite understand why you young men of rank should be so prejudiced in my favour. I suspect it's more to do with fashion than any special merit of mine. Flattered as I am, I am heart-whole, and it's a heavy price to pay if I have to condole all morning with one fool and spend the long evening sympathising with another! I can't be tender and true to a dozen of you at a time.'

Worcester was hurt. 'I didn't know I was quite a fool and, if I am, I shan't intrude my folly on you any further.'

He picked up his hat again, put it on and pulled it down in a vain attempt to hide his tears.

'What am I to do, Lord Worcester?' said Harriette, spreading her hands. 'I can't bear to make people who love me unhappy! I'd make you and Leinster and my sister Fanny all happy if I could – provided they don't grow *too* pathetic.'

'My dear, dearest Harriette,' said Worcester, 'no man on earth, feeling the way I do, could have been less pathetic! For the last six months all my prayers, all my hopes, all my wishes, have been for you and your happiness. I've visited you seldom and I've never done anything to bore or offend you.'

'True,' admitted Harriette.

'Well, then,' cried the lad, 'I'll throw myself on my knees —'

'Please don't! I really must go to Astley's; there's not a moment to lose. I've promised to go out with Leinster, but I believe you love me more than he's capable of loving anything or anybody, and, since you are kind enough to value my friendship, I won't cut you out of my life.'

She held out her hand, which he covered with warm kisses and warmer tears.

'You must go now,' she added. 'I never break my word, and Leinster will be here in a minute. But when he goes to Spain —'

'Is he really going?' interrupted Worcester.

'Oh yes, it's all settled. In less than six weeks, he won't be here to torment you.'

Worcester was overjoyed.

'And when he's gone, there won't be a man you care about left in England?'

'Nobody! I've a sort of tenderness, nothing like a passion, for Lord Robert Manners; I've a great respect for Lord Frederick Bentinck's morals – and that's all! So now, my lord, you must set off; and do be merry! You'll hear from me often and as soon as Leinster's gone you're welcome to try and make me in love with you.'

'I'm not to call on you till then?' pouted the boy.

'I'll write and tell you all about it.'

There was a loud rap at the door.

'I'm off,' said Worcester. 'I can't bear to sit here with Leinster for a single minute.' He added in French, 'I beg you, my angel, have pity on me, and don't forget me.' He dropped on one knee to kiss her hand, like a knight of old, and the next instant he was gone.

'Was that the Marquis of Worcester running out of your home in such a hurry as I was getting out of my carriage?' asked Leinster, as he entered the room, in full evening dress. Harriette could not help admiring his handsome legs, set off to the best advantage by fine silk stockings.

'Yes,' said Harriette, 'but I've asked him not to come again, so please don't be sentimental. I've had enough of that today to last me for life.'

'You are very cold and heartless, which I never suspected,' said Leinster.

'I was enough in love once, God knows,' sighed Harriette, 'and what good did it do me?'

Astley's was well attended. Harriette thought she glimpsed Worcester through the trellis-work of a stage box, but could not be certain. After the show, Harriette wanted to say goodnight to the Duke of Leinster at his own door, but he insisted that he was starving, and said nothing would do but a thick slice of bread and butter. This luxury, together with a tankard of ale, was procured by his footman from a public house near the theatre, keeping Harriette waiting.

Next morning Harriette's darling sister Fanny came to say goodbye; Colonel Parker was leaving for Portsmouth, where his regiment was stationed.

'Remember me to Lord Worcester, when you see him,' said Fanny. 'There is something in that young man's countenance I like so much, and his manners are so extremely high-bred and gentlemanly, that I can't think how you can resist him and treat him so very coldly. Amy is desperate to be introduced to him.'

Julia had overcome her dislike of Napier, and had become almost as fond of him as she had been of Sir Harry Mildmay. This was the reason she had not gone to Brighton with Harriette and her sisters.

'Does Napier treat Julia and her family well?'

'He's horribly stingy,' replied Fanny. 'Julia has to appear cold and refuse him the slightest favour till he brings her money; otherwise she'd get nothing out of him. Yet he seems passionately fond of her, and writes sonnets on her beauty, describing her – in her mid-thirties and mother of nine children – as his "beautiful maid".'[4]

Fanny's chariot was at the door, so the sisters went to visit Julia. Julia had recently had a miscarriage, and was gracefully reclining on her chaise-longue, elegantly dressed, while Sophia hammered at a little country dance on the pianoforte. Sophia's admirer, Harriette learned, was Lord Berwick[5]. Berwick was a nervous, selfish, odd man, afraid of driving his own horses, so he had come to an arrangement with the impecunious Lord William Somerset, uncle to

Lord Worcester, and in Holy Orders. Lord William, brother of the rich Duke of Beaufort, was like other younger sons in having a title but no means, and was therefore forced into a church sinecure to ensure a modest stipend. So Lord William, who enjoyed driving and opportunities for borrowing from his wealthy employer, became Lord Berwick's driver or 'tiger'. Berwick said to Lord William: 'I've at last found a woman I should like to marry, Somerset, and I've been on the look-out for more than twenty years.'

'Who is she?'

Berwick described Sophia.

'I think I know who you mean, since you mention the house. It belongs to Miss Storer, Lord Carysfort's niece, who has, I know, a fine young girl staying with her, the one Lord Deerhurst seduced.'

'Seduced already! You don't say so!'

'Quite true, my lord,' said 'Tiger' Somerset. 'I've often seen her out with Deerhurst last year. She hasn't any eyebrows –'

'I don't care a damn about eyebrows, and I'll have her,' said Lord Berwick. So Lord William Somerset presented Lord Berwick to Sophia. Lord William had asked Julia's permission to present him, and Berwick was a man of fortune and great respectability. Fanny and Harriette wished Sophia joy and kissed her.

The parting with Fanny, who was leaving to live with Colonel Parker in Portsmouth, hit Harriette hard. Fanny, she was convinced, was the only sister who cared about her, and they had only rarely been separated. They agreed to correspond regularly and Harriette promised that, if Fanny had a spare bed, she would visit. Fanny said: 'Tell me all about Lord Worcester. It's lucky for Colonel Parker that Lord Worcester never turned an eye of love on me.'

Harriette came home feeling low and was told that Leinster, who had been waiting for her more than an hour, had just gone, but a ladylike young Frenchwoman was still in Harriette's dressing room. She had come to offer her services in the place of Harriette's previous paid companion, Miss Eliza Higgins. Harriette liked the young woman on sight: she seemed modest, quiet and unaffected; she looked about twenty, but said she was twenty-five. Her previous employer had been Lady Caroline Lamb. Harriette engaged her at once without taking up references.

She passed a restless night, tormented by a craving for love. What could I not have been and done, she thought, for the friend, the companion, the husband of my choice? She was nearly twenty-seven. Lord Worcester, she reflected, knew how to love, which was something, but where was the magic of the mind, the intellect she hungered to respect?

The new French maid next morning brought her an enormously long letter from Lord Worcester, which she showed to the writer Henry Luttrell when he called early.

'Does this young man love me?' she asked wistfully.

'With all his soul, his heart and his strength,' was the reply.

Harriette wrote to Fanny, enclosing Worcester's letter, and passing on scandalous gossip about Lady Caroline Lamb and the doctor who attended her sickly son. Lady Caroline, said her former employee, whose name was Thérèse, was always trying to persuade her servants that sleep was unnecessary, merely a matter of habit. She often called them up in the night to listen to her performance on the organ. Her ladyship's poetry, said Thérèse, was equally good, in French, in English, or in Italian; she was also a gifted caricaturist. She sacked her servants according to whim, without reason. Harriette also reported to Fanny that Alvanley was so deep in debt that his horses had been impounded; he had had the knocker taken off his door because the duns prevented him sleeping in the mornings. 'Brummell they say is entirely ruined,' she added.

'Lord Berwick teases Julia and me from morning to night,' wrote Harriette. 'He wants us to persuade Sophia to receive a settlement from him of five hundred a year, and to place herself under his protection. We do not like to advise at all on such subjects; and whenever he ventures to touch on them to Sophia herself, she begins to sob and cry as if she were threatened with sudden death! I asked her last night why she accepted so many magnificent presents from his lordship and suffered him to put himself to such immense expense if she disliked him so violently.'

'Oh, I never said I disliked his carriages, or his jewels, or his nice dinners,' answered Sophia. In Sophia's opinion, Lord Berwick, then in his early forties, was both old and boring, but on the second day she agreed to go for a drive in his luxurious barouche, although she declared she found him repulsive. She refused to be alone with him, though she ate his dinners.

Worcester was asked to join them but refused to go anywhere without Harriette, so Harriette's time was taken up playing chaperone. The Duke of Leinster was about to leave for Spain, and Lord Worcester's joy was so transparent that he was laughed at in White's Club. He had just joined the 10th Hussars at Brighton and implored Harriette to go with him. This crack regiment had been raised in 1715 and fought in the Seven Years' War. When the war with France began in 1793, the regiment was gazetted as 'the 10th, or Prince of Wales' Own Regiment of Light Dragoons' and in 1796 the Prince was appointed Colonel-in-Chief. In 1811 the Prince changed the name to 'The Prince of Wales's Own Royal Regiment of Hussars'. Brummell had spent a short period as junior officer with them.

Lord Berwick wanted to take a fine house at Brighton for Sophia and Julia, sending down his plate and his chef. Sophia said he could hire a grand house if he liked, but she preferred to go on living with Julia in a smaller one. She announced she would continue to accept invitations to dinner parties at Berwick's house in Grosvenor Square, however, so long as Harriette and Worcester were present.This made Harriette feel she was being manipulated, as

Sophia seemed to be throwing them together. Generally she met Worcester at houses other than her own, but when Harriette's asthma returned, Worcester nursed her tenderly, running up and down from kitchen to drawing room, pouring her water gruel and her tea, keeping at a respectful emotional distance. Harriette was touched by his devotion, but it found no answering spark. She brooded that she was tired of flattery and her self-esteem was at a low ebb; if she was as bewitching as people told her she was, why had Ponsonby abandoned her, leaving her in despair? She told Fanny the world trampled on her. Worcester meanwhile promised he would never marry anybody else.

Fanny replied that she thought Worcester the most interesting man she knew. Fanny had become pregnant by Parker, who was delighted. Ladies in Portsmouth, who believed Fanny to be his wife, gave them invitations which Fanny was squeamish about accepting. Harriette advised her to accept. Fanny, besotted with Parker, gently refused advances from other men. Amy had tried to win Parker away from Fanny, without success, and was making advances to Worcester. Worcester ignored her and asked Julia about his chances of persuading Harriette to go with him to Brighton. Fanny ruptured a blood vessel and Harriette rushed to Portsmouth, where she was living in a pretty cottage, to visit her.

Leinster was there, waiting to sail for Spain. Parker was away and Fanny invited Leinster to dinner, although she did not like him and despised him as 'stupid'. Harriette could only compare Leinster unfavourably to Worcester, who wrote her immensely long letters. Fanny said it was selfish of Leinster not to enquire about Harriette's finances. Instead of walking with Harriette, he went sailing every morning, which stung Harriette's pride. Harriette disliked and despised Leinster as a fool, yet characteristically expected to milk him for money. Returned to her house, she tells us she found numerous cards and letters and another plain envelope containing another £200. Clearly she is less than frank about this period of her life. How did she pay the rent? Such large anonymous donations of £200 seem improbable; presumably Leinster was keeping her.

Julia called next morning. She reported that Amy had met a woman who had had an affair with the Honourable John Ward. He had been all fire and ice; on going to bed, he demanded three extra blankets, but after fifteen minutes decided he had a fever, threw off all the bedclothes and opened the window, and was soon shivering again.

Julia was concerned for Harriette's welfare.

'Do go to Brighton,' she urged. 'You'll never find anybody to like you as I'm sure Lord Worcester does. I wouldn't advise you, if I didn't think he deserved you.'

'I'll think about it,' said Harriette. 'In the meantime, please tell me some news. How does Lord Berwick go on?'

'He's as much in love with Sophia as ever.'

'And Sophia?'

'Oh, she hates him more than ever and says she won't go to Brighton unless you decide to go there with Lord Worcester.'

Worcester shortly arrived and, entreated by him, pressed by Julia, inclined by gratitude and by asthma, but without being at all in love, Harriette agreed to place herself under the protection of the Marquis of Worcester, aged nineteen.

Notes to Chapter Eight

1. Page 95: It is not altogether clear what Miss Higgins's duties as paid companion would have been. Harriette at various times mentions a lady's maid and a footman, but we do not know how many servants she employed at various times in her chequered career.

2. Page 97: Lord Robert Manners (1781–1835), paid to be left off the list of Harriette's lovers.

3. Page 100: In those days, the age of majority was twenty-one.

4. Page 102: Harriette says that Julia was twenty-five when they met, which was when Harriette was with Fred Lamb, presumably soon after 1802. Writing of 1811–12, she says Julia was forty! No wonder Julia was enraged.

5. Page 102: Thomas Noel Hill, second Baron Berwick (1770–1832). He was forty-two when he married Sophia, who was fifteen. Despite the assertion she had 'his eyebrows', in her portrait (p69) they are clearly marked.

9

At Home with the Marquis of Worcester

Lord Berwick's carriage with four magnificent horses led the way to Brighton, followed by humbler vehicles carrying his cook, his frying pans and the rest of his kitchen gear. After a decent interval Julia and Sophia started out in a neat little chariot drawn by two scraggy horses, because Sophia intended to advertise her somewhat shaky virtue by travelling separately from Berwick, with a female chaperone. Harriette had sent Lord Worcester down alone so he could take a house and have everything ready.

'But when I've joined my regiment I shan't be allowed to return,' complained Worcester.

'That doesn't matter,' said Harriette. 'My maid and I can find our way to Brighton in perfect safety.'

'I can ride ten or fifteen miles to meet you,' said Worcester.

Harriette was tempted not to go, but she had given her word and her maid had started packing. As the carriage approached Brighton, Worcester rode up to them; this was the first time Harriette had seen him in uniform. The costume was dashing; officers wore laced jackets, sashes, fur caps, and red breeches with gold fringe, giving rise to the nickname of 'cherry bums' or – more politely – 'cherubim'. Being a cavalry regiment, it drew heavily on the nobility, and ordered them to grow moustaches. Harriette remained unimpressed: she decided, for the moment, that a gentleman always looked better in plain clothes.

Worcester had taken a house in Rock Gardens, where he had left his footman, Mr Will Haught, to get 'all square'. This was Mr Haught's favourite expression. He was a stiff, grave, steady person of about forty. He always wore the Beaufort livery, and on Sundays used to sit in the hall reading the Bible, with a clean pocket handkerchief tied round his head to prevent his catching cold. Harriette suspected that the pious Duchess of Beaufort had set him to watch over the morals of the young heir, together with a coachman, groom, undergroom and a soldier who took his lordship's horse to the stable. What a bore it'll be to have all these lazy, beer-drinking men in the house, thought Harriette, unused to the ducal style of living. Haught had hired a female servant who was introduced to Harriette as her own maid.

Worcester was overjoyed to have Harriette to himself at last.

'I've been terrified of losing you,' he said, kissing Harriette's hand, and then he burst into tears. Sniffing and scrubbing his eyes, he said with gentle courtesy,

'You've had a long journey. Would you prefer to pass this first night alone?'

'Where are you to sleep, then?'

'Oh, there's a good bed in my dressing room, of course,' said Worcester, surprised at the middle-class notion that a couple might have only one bed.

Harriette was impressed by such a scale of housekeeping and touched at such consideration. 'If you'll let me spend tonight alone, I shall be full of *joie-de-vivre* tomorrow,' she promised. 'Everything here is a little strange to me so, if I am a little melancholy, you mustn't imagine it's from any lack of regard for you.'

An excellent dinner was served and during the meal Worcester said, 'By the way, my love, Tweed wanted to dine with us, along with Mrs Cotton and Miss Sophia Dubochet, but I didn't presume to invite them until I knew it would be agreeable to you.'

'Tweed?'

'Lord Berwick.'

'Oh.'

Lord Worcester's tall figure looked remarkably handsome in the elegant evening uniform of the 10th Hussars, and Harriette was so moved by his courtly deference to her that when he handed her to the bedroom with a kiss on the forehead and a gentle 'Goodnight and sleep well, my sweet' she half regretted having expressed a wish to sleep alone.

'It's a nice room and there's a good fire burning,' she said brightly. 'Do you think there are any ghosts in this part of the world?'

Worcester was too shy to take this hint.

'I'm close at hand,' he said. 'I shall be with you in an instant if you just touch the bell.'

Harriette slept well in the luxurious feather bed. She was woken by the voice of Lord Berwick calling to Worcester from outdoors.

'Brought you some apples,' he shouted. 'Came from my country house this morning. Sophia wants the pair of you to come to dinner with me today; won't come unless you do.'

Harriette slipped on a dressing gown and told Lord Berwick through the window that she would meet her sister with pleasure.

'I ought to be on parade,' said Worcester. 'But whatever happens to me, darling Harriette, I promise never to leave you, ever.'

After breakfast, his two grooms rode up to the door with three horses.

'Who's going to ride the one without a saddle?' wondered Harriette.

Worcester sent Will Haught up to his dressing room to fetch a beautiful side-saddle, embroidered with blue silk. Worcester invited her to ride: 'I chose this saddle myself and it will always be kept in my dressing room, so nobody but you may use it.'

They took a long ride and met Colonel Palmer, a former acquaintance of

Harriette's, who invited her to dine in the mess with Lord Worcester.

'Not today,' said Harriette, 'but certainly next week, with Worcester's permission.'

They settled a day early in the following week and Colonel Palmer said he would arrange for dinner to be delayed an hour, knowing how the aristocratic Worcester preferred to eat late.

Harriette Wilson takes
a morning gallop at Brighton

'By the way,' said Colonel Palmer, 'Colonel Quentin[1] is not very pleased that Lord Worcester missed parade this morning. I shall scold *you*, madam, if it happens again.' In 1815, Colonel (later Sir) George Quentin and Colonel Charles Palmer were to fight a duel; neither was hurt, but Quentin was later wounded at the battle of Waterloo.

Worcester, Harriette and Colonel Palmer rode for most of the day. The under-groom, who was waiting at the door for Harriette's horse, held out his hand for her foot, to help her dismount while Worcester was saying goodbye to the Colonel. Harriette was about to accept when Worcester, much agitated, told the man to desist and never to attempt such presumption again. He helped Harriette down himself.

'I shan't like you any the better for getting your gloves dirty with my muddy shoes, you know,' she murmured.

'The fellow had no right,' insisted Worcester.

Lord Berwick laid on a magnificent dinner, but Sophia snapped irritably at him throughout. After dinner they played cards, which bored Harriette; she did not enjoy her evening.

That night Worcester took her to bed. At nineteen, he was no virgin. Oxford in 1811 had no women's colleges, but the city swarmed with prostitutes to service the young men and Worcester had early contracted a venereal disease. His mother read him lectures and told him his dose was a punishment from God. Worcester laughed; he did not believe God cared one way or the other. Despite his early experiments with low women, he was fastidious and even in his way ambitious; from early teens he had heard, at Oatlands and elsewhere, of the legendary charms of Miss Wilson, and he had laid plans to possess her. Everyone in his circle knew her. He was used to having the best of everything; he could afford it. Having obtained possession, he was in the seventh heaven. This was the honeymoon of his dreams.

Undressing her, he observed that her small pink nipples were as delectable as he had heard. He trembled as his penis touched her and, to his embarrassment, exploded. Harriette laughed gently.

'No matter, my lord,' she said, taking him in hand. 'We have all the time in the world.'

'Call me Henry, darling,' said Worcester.

But Harriette enjoyed using a title in intimate circumstances. She taught him to give pleasure as well as taking it, together with all the tricks of her trade. If true love was missing, physical satisfaction was better than nothing, she told herself. His virility consoled her for the passion which on her side was lacking and she grew fond of him in the way an older woman may feel for a novice lover. And she was living in unprecedented comfort, even grandeur. Worcester, a high-bred gentleman, cosseted her as nobody else ever had or would. When she consulted a doctor about a minor ailment, Worcester wrote the doctor an extravagant letter, enclosing a £50 note, saying he would be grateful for ever if treatment were of the slightest use. He sent servants running after her with winter shoes and fur cloaks on fine days, in case it should rain. He supervised the housekeeping, ordering dinner himself, because Harriette liked it to be a surprise. Every morning he got out of bed to make toast at the bedroom fire for her, saying it was cleaner than if the footman had touched it. He laced up her stays, singing a little song in a mock Cockney accent: 'Broken-hearted I vanders … '[2].

Lord Berwick, a quarter of a century older than Sophia, urged Harriette to persuade Sophia to live with him, offering Sophia an annuity of £500.

The Marquis of Worcester made breakfast toast himself and laced up Harriette's stays

'But she doesn't like you.'

'If I give her whatever she wants, she may get over her dislike.'

'Is it her beauty that appeals to you?'

Sophia, younger sister, was the comparatively plain one.

'Partly that,' answered Berwick solemnly. 'More to the point, though, she always tells the truth.'

'She tells you the truth about liking the good things your money can buy, and she's honest enough to say she doesn't care for you! She's especially fond of a good dinner —'

'Then you ought to advise her to come to me! I want to get a house for her in town and furnish it.'

'I won't interfere,' said Harriette.

In the evening they all – Julia, Sophia, Harriette and Worcester – went to Lord Berwick's private box at the theatre and were very merry, except for Berwick himself. He sat at the back of the box, where he could neither see nor hear. Sophia ignored him. Harriette felt uncomfortable that her host should be so miserably placed.

'I assure you I'd rather sit in the dark than watch a play,' he said.

'Sophia ought to chat with you, then.'

'I don't like being talked to. But I don't think Sophia will ever deceive me.'

The day fixed for dining in the mess arrived. Harriette knew some of the officers already, and – skilled observer that she was – kept a shrewd eye on their interactions. She could see that a very handsome young officer who was rich, but of inferior birth, was totally ignored by his fellows, and pretended not to notice. Captain FitzClarence, bastard son of the Duke of Clarence and Mrs Jordan the actress, was fined for coming in to dinner with dirty boots, his dirty habits and his greed, coupled with arrogance and conceit about his royal connexions, made him unpopular.

Lord Worcester was severely reprimanded for missing parade the previous week. Colonel Palmer scolded Harriette and threatened that punishment would follow if Worcester did it again. After dinner, Harriette warned Worcester that he really had to be there at eight o'clock the next morning. The lovesick lad promised, but, exhausted by romping in bed with Harriette, did not turn up. He was arrested and forbidden to wear his sword.

'By God, if he was the king's son, I'd put him under arrest,' growled Colonel Quentin.

Lord Worcester, hearing of this remark, loftily dismissed it as vulgar: 'What has a king's son or a duke's son to do with the usual discipline observed towards lieutenants in the army?'

Eventually arrangements were made for the couple to breakfast at the barracks. Harriette wore a blue riding habit, an embroidered jacket with the regimental trim and a little grey fur cap with a gold band. Young Edward

Fitzgerald, cousin to the Duke of Leinster, galloped after the pair and said to Worcester: 'There's a damned old fellow has been telling everybody about you being put under arrest and having your sword taken from you for making such a fool of yourself about Harriette.'

Worcester went red with anger. 'I must take the liberty, Fitzgerald, of reminding you that the lady you call Harriette I consider as my wife. You will offend me if ever you treat her with less respect than you would show to the Marchioness of Worcester, and I am sure you will desist from calling her by her Christian name.' Fitzgerald apologized for his thoughtlessness.

Harriette watched the drill from Worcester's barrack room and listened to Sergeant Whitaker teach the sword exercise, which she brilliantly records for us:

'Tik nuttiss! The wurd dror is oney a carshun. At t'wurd suards, ye drors um hout, tekin a farm un positif grip o' the hilt! Sem time, throwing the shith smartly backords thus! Dror! Steady there! Never a finger or a heye to move i' the head. Dror suards!'

Fanny, now mother of a little girl by Parker, arrived on a visit, and Worcester and Harriette entertained her with Julia, Sophia and Lord Berwick. Julia was planning to join Napier in Leicestershire.

The ladies withdrew after dinner. Fanny told Sophia she was treating Berwick badly in taking so much from him and giving nothing in return. Sophia began to cry.

'It seems to make no difference to you whether your lover is old or young, handsome or ugly, provided he gives you things. You must be the coldest girl in England; you've never had a sensation in your life,' teased Fanny.

'What do you call a sensation?'

'Well,' said Fanny, 'you seem to feel exactly the same in the company of men as in that of women.'

'How do you know?'

Pressed to explain, Sophia said: 'Well, then, you remember the handsome young cobbler, who lived in Chapel Street? Used to make my shoes? I was always dropping in on some pretext or other, like asking when they'd be ready, and taking my old ones to him to be mended. One day he touched my hand. I believe he was nervous, but it was very pleasant. Finding that I didn't resent this first liberty, he began to kiss me, and I didn't know how to push him away or what to say.'

'What next?' laughed the others, drawing up their chairs.

Sophia blushed and hesitated. 'The next thing was — uh — very nasty indeed,' she said.

'What thing do you mean?'

'A very shocking one.'

'How do you mean, shocking?'

'Come on,' said Julia. 'Out with it.'

'That's what happened,' said Sophia.

'You don't mean to say he —'

'That's what he did.'

'And that's the only time you've felt a sensation?' said Harriette.

'Well, I never felt so strange before,' said Sophia.

'What did you do?'

'I was running out of the shop; my face must have been scarlet. I was only thirteen at the time.'

'So what prevented you?'

'The cobbler. He took my hand and made me touch him, saying there was nothing to be afraid of, as it was quite clean.'

The other women convulsed.

'I got away as fast as I could, but it was a week before I got the cobbler out of my head. Don't tell Lord Berwick.'

Mischievous Fanny solemnly told her sister that she would be unable to resist doing so. When the men came upstairs Fanny said that Sophia had once had a romance with a cobbler, and Lord Berwick said he would have no peace till he had heard all about it. Fanny built up the story as a grand mystery and refused to reveal details, while Sophia sat blushing and fanning herself.

Sophia gave Berwick a hint that he could hope. A month later he fitted up a nice house for her in London's Montagu Square, and Sophia, after stipulating that she should sleep alone for a few weeks, went with him.

Worcester was more and more infatuated with Harriette. When she had a molar extracted, he wore it round his neck; he grew anxious when she was out of his sight; he refused all invitations for six months, and ate every night with Harriette. His paternal uncle, Lord Charles Somerset, grew angry and threatened to tell Worcester's parents. It was ridiculous for a man of Worcester's high rank to seclude himself like a hermit, said Lord Charles. He hoped Worcester would not fail to be present at his uncle's birthday party. Harriette persuaded him he ought to go.

'My dearest Harriette,' said Worcester, 'having bound myself to you for life, for better or worse, and with my eyes open, I hate going anywhere you can't come with me.'

Harriette pleaded delicate health. Having arranged for Harriette to have an early dinner, at the last minute Worcester rebelled: why should he be a slave to Charles Somerset? His carriage was brought to the door, but he sent it away and ordered cold beef for his own supper.

'What'll you say to your uncle?' asked Harriette.

'Uncle be hanged!' retorted the nephew.

It was after ten when Lord Charles sent a groom on horseback to enquire for Worcester. The young man ran up to the bedroom, put on his night-cap, and called down through the window that he was ill in bed and not to be disturbed.

When the Prince Regent, whose regiment the 10th Hussars was, came to the Brighton Pavilion, and invited the officers to dine, Worcester could not get out of it. He said goodbye to Harriette as romantically as if he were leaving for Australia. The Prince courteously gave this well-born young man a general invitation for the evenings and Worcester was forced to pretend he had sprained his ankle.

Eventually Worcester's solicitude and possessiveness began to get on Harriette's nerves. When Fanny went to join Colonel Parker in London, Harriette begged for a week away. Worcester attempted to bribe Colonel Quentin with cigars into letting him take a week off as well, but, although the Colonel took the gift, permission was refused. Worcester was tempted to ask for his cigars back, but was too well bred to do so.

Fanny and Harriette found Sophia very comfortably set up, in a good house and a handsome carriage, still keeping Lord Berwick at arm's length. They drove to Julia's, and learned that Julia had received several hundred pounds in ready money for having coaxed Sophia into living in the same house, if not sleeping in the same bed, with Lord Berwick.

Harriette sighed. 'Well,' she said acidly, 'you have a large family. However, I'm still too young to take up this new profession of yours, Julia.'

Julia was stung: 'I acted responsibly, in Sophia's own interests. I believe he intends to marry her, you know.'

'I won't have him,' said Sophia.

'Why not?' chorused the three demi-reps, Julia, Fanny and Harriette. Because, Sophia said, it was a shocking thing to swear to love only one man. They teased her about the amorous cobbler.

'I'm sorry I told you. I shall never hear the last of it. Julia hasn't only told Lord Berwick; she's made it out worse than it is.'

'I can't *think* how she could manage that,' said Fanny.

Sophia entertained them all, together with Lord Berwick, to dinner. Lord Berwick wondered how many men had been cuckolded in London that season; recreational sex is no twentieth-century innovation.

'I neither know nor care,' said Harriette. 'By the way, Sophia, what has become of Lord Deerhurst's valuable jewels?'

'Oh, I quite forgot about them.'

'Do let me see them,' said Lord Berwick. He roared with laughter at the thought of his beloved Sophia having been seduced by Lord Deerhurst on the strength of such trash. The 'jewellery' was returned to Deerhurst with a polite note.

After dinner, Berwick urged Sophia to marry him. At first she refused, then weakened so far as to say she would consider it.

'This house is so beautifully fitted up, even to the very attics, that it would be a pity to leave it,' said Fanny.

'Can't be helped,' said Lord Berwick cheerfully. 'We'll have to sell it, for of course Lady Berwick must live in my family house in Grosvenor Square.'

Next morning came a characteristically long letter from Worcester. Lord Charles Somerset had written to his brother the Duke of Beaufort, with the result that the Duke and Duchess had written severe letters to their son, insisting that he abandon his mistress at once. Worcester assured Harriette that nothing, not even infidelity on her part, could induce him to leave her. He only wished he were twenty-one instead of twenty, so that he could marry her legally without the consent of his parents, but he would soon be of age. He sent his love to Fanny and Sophia, whom he regarded already as sisters, and implored Harriette to be his wife. Harriette begged him, in her reply, not to irritate his parents unnecessarily. The question of marriage she avoided, but assured him of her loyalty and said she would never willingly cause him a moment's pain. She promised to return to Brighton in three days' time. Being followed in the street by a mysterious, silent man, she left earlier, suspecting he had been set on to her by the Beauforts.

Harriette knew how to keep up appearances, but Worcester had grand notions in accordance with his social position, and scorned economy, equating it with meanness. She refused to accept jewels, except a pair of pink topaz earrings, which cost less than thirty guineas. He borrowed thousands at exorbitant interest, refusing to let her interfere. When the Duke of Beaufort found out the terms, he threatened the moneylender with prosecution for fraud on a minor if he did not sign a receipt in full for the bare sum lent; Harriette considered this to be sharp practice on the part of the Duke. Harriette and Worcester were tired of Brighton, and Worcester was tired of the army. As heir to the Badminton estate, he did not need a profession, although his father believed and hoped that young men were improved by military service. Worcester confessed to Harriette that he had joined chiefly in the hope that she would find him irresistible in uniform.

Sophia agreed to marry Berwick. She had – in Harriette's words – 'thrown herself into the arms of a debauchee at thirteen with her eyes open, then offered herself for sale to Colonel Berkeley', and when her terms were 'refused with scorn and contempt by the handsome and young' accepted, at fifteen, 'age and ugliness for a yearly stipend, and at length, by good luck, without one atom of virtue, became a wife.'

The night before Sophia's wedding, her father was able to boast to a malicious neighbour of his daughter's coup. She married Lord Berwick on 8 February 1812 and died at Leamington in 1875, having survived her husband by forty-three years. Harriette's memoir makes her out to be foolish, but she brought off a coup which neither Julia, nor Fanny, nor Harriette, nor Amy could match; she married, legally – and, moreover, into the peerage. Her husband made it a condition that she cut off all contact with her relatives, even her gentle mother, though secretly Sophia remained in touch with kindly Fanny until Fanny's early death. Sophia squandered Berwick's money recklessly, sometimes on gifts to the poor. When the house in Montagu Square was sold for two thousand pounds, and the agent presented Sophia with the cash, she sent it to her mother. We may perhaps approve of this generosity, but Harriette considered it foolish. After a year Lord Berwick was in hock to his creditors. Sophia, covered in diamonds, looked splendid in her opera box, where she was ogled by Lord Deerhurst, who winked at his friends in order to annoy Lord Berwick[3].

The baby of the Dubochet family was Charlotte, then seven, a beauty and a promising dancer. She was already on the stage, when Lord and Lady Berwick chose, says Harriette, to 'rescue her from a profession where her talents might have made her a fortune' and enhanced her prospects of marrying well. Charlotte went to live with the nobility, who made a pet of her. She attracted eligible young men, which irritated Sophia into packing her off to earn her living as a teacher in a country school.

'Patronage is a fine thing!' writes Harriette savagely. 'I should like to know what Charlotte says about it as she sits darning her cotton stockings on a Saturday night.'

Sophia's treatment of Charlotte was possibly less brutal than Harriette is willing to admit. A letter to a newspaper in 1825 said that 'Charlotte, who is very beautiful, but has the misfortune to be lame, lives in retirement with an elder sister in a small and obscure lodging in Church Street, Paddington, where Lady B visits them and supplies their wants.' Probably it was illness or accident rather than harsh treatment by Lord and Lady Berwick that ended Charlotte's stage career. Harriette found Sophia's spectacularly grand marriage hard to forgive.

Not that their path was entirely smooth: Lord Berwick threw a hot leg of mutton at the footman's head because it was served without a paper frill; Sophia fretted because the hairdresser cut her hair too short in front. Sophia complained a great deal, but was on the whole satisfied with her lot in life, as well she might be.

The Beauforts, terrified that their son might make a harlot into a Marchioness, kept bombarding Worcester with orders to leave Harriette. He swore daily he would make her his wife. The Duchess did not mince her words: 'This absurd attachment of yours for this vile profligate woman does but prove the total subjugation of your understanding,' she wrote. The Duke wrote insisting that Worcester join him at once at the family seat. Another uncle, Lord William Somerset – Lord Berwick's driver or 'tiger' – turned up and would not leave until he had seen Worcester, in floods of tears, safely into the Oxford mail coach at seven-thirty in the evening. As Harriette said, what was an extravagant fellow like Lord William, with high rank and no money, to do? He mocked poor Worcester's romance and made a pass at Harriette himself. Harriette laughed at him, but decided she liked him best of the whole set.

Colonel Parker was off to Spain and Fanny was depressed. She went back to being Julia's lodger. Worcester's enormously long letters came every day. He said his father had given permission for him to return to Harriette, but had demanded a promise that he would never marry her. Worcester came back and the couple lived peaceably together in London, Worcester more defiant than ever and begging Harriette to marry him at Gretna Green[4].

Harriette teased Worcester that Lord Frederick Beauclerc, another younger son who had entered the church, had agreed to perform the marriage ceremony for Worcester and Harriette, on condition he enjoyed *les droits du seigneur*. Worcester was puzzled; he did not understand.

'It means the bridegroom's privilege on the first night,' said Harriette solemnly. Worcester, realising he was being mocked, was hurt and offended.

The Beauforts' nightmare was that the couple might be married already. Harriette and Worcester returned to Brighton for a couple of months, until Worcester's regiment was sent to Portsmouth to guard prisoners of war. He told her constantly that he adored her. For him she felt a sisterly fondness, having become used to his constant kind attention and elegant manners. When Worcester's army leave was due, the Duke of Beaufort insisted on his son's presence at Badminton and the lad obeyed. Harriette went back to her London house.

A pathetic letter arrived from Worcester, who complained that his parents were detaining him. His mother claimed to be ill and his father insisted that she would never recover from her last confinement while her mind was so dreadfully agitated. 'I can neither eat nor sleep, and both my father and uncle admit that they have tormented me till I am seriously ill. I implore you then, my adored, beloved darling Harriette, to come to me. I never close my eyes in sleep without waking in the greatest fright and agony, having dreamed that you were taken away from me for ever … '

Worcester hatched a plot whereby he would sneak out of his bed to an inn at Oxford to meet Harriette – who would travel in disguise – at midnight. Harriette decked herself up as a countrywoman in thick shoes, blue stockings, blue check apron, coloured neckerchief, cloth cap and bright cherry-coloured ribbons. She travelled from London by stage-coach, in company far from elegant. Once arrived, she realised she had got on the wrong coach, as the inn mentioned by Worcester was a mile away, and it was pouring with rain. Eventually she found a working man willing to take her there, although he was suspicious when this humbly-dressed woman offered him a generous tip of half a crown ($12^{1}/_{2}$p). Worcester was waiting eagerly at the door but failed to recognize the bedraggled 'country girl' and pushed her roughly aside until she spoke.

'Good God, my love! How came you alone this miserable night?' he said, his manner totally altered.

He handed her upstairs, all joy and rapture and trembling anxiety lest she had caught cold. In less than fifteen minutes she was in a warm bed with an excellent supper alongside. They talked all night long.

'I shall have no peace of mind till we are really married,' he said.

'Your father would never forgive you.'

'That I shall deeply regret, but I must and will choose my partner for life. You and I have passed weeks, months, years together, without having had a single quarrel. Harmony of temper between man and wife is the greatest blessing in marriage.'

Harriette could only agree.

'I was never happy till I knew you,' said Worcester. 'I'm quite sure that you are the only woman on earth I could be faithful to for life. My father will have to submit in the end.'

'Your parents may be harsh, but I shan't give them reason to curse me. It can't be. By making me your wife you lose them for ever. Let's just make the best of the present moment.'

They made love several times that night. At nine next morning Worcester called a cab so that Harriette, disguised as a servant, would not be spoken to familiarly by strangers. A mile out of Oxford Lord Edward Somerset[5], another of Worcester's uncles, passed and stared hard at Harriette, who hoped her disguise was impenetrable. But she was recognized; Worcester wrote to her saying she had been seen in a 'very odd, unladylike kind of dress' near Oxford. The Duke and Duchess had laughed at him as the dupe of a wicked woman, who was moreover 'deformed and ugly', he reported. Tact was not young Worcester's strong point.

A Mr Meyler was currently a guest of the Duchess of Beaufort; dismissed by Lord Alvanley as a mere 'sugar-baker', he owned property in the West Indies that brought in between £25,000 and £35,000 a year. He was a little over twenty-one and, Harriette heard, very handsome. She also heard that he had assured the Duchess no man in his right mind could be in love with Harriette.

'You know her, then?' said the Duchess.

'I've never spoken to her,' admitted Meyler, 'but I see her every night in her opera box and in the round room afterwards; I know all about her.'

Colonel Berkeley was spreading a rumour that he and his brother Augustus had both slept with Harriette and Worcester asked her if it were true. Indeed, it may well have been, but Harriette denied it. Worcester's devotion was beginning to bore and cloy; Harriette could see no future in the relationship, though had she been more astute she might have become Duchess of Beaufort. She decided to pursue Meyler[6].

Notes to Chapter Nine

1. Page 110: Because 'Quentin' is pronounced 'Quinton', the Colonel's name is variously spelt in the Army Lists.

2. Page 111: Worcester follows the eighteenth and nineteenth century Cockneyism of inverting 'v' and 'w'. The song was a popular ballad of the period, with the chorus: 'Broken-hearted I'll wander, broken-hearted I'll remain, | Since my bonny light horseman in the wars he was slain.' Lord Worcester may have heard some of his hussars singing it. Hussars, along with lancers, are 'light horsemen', as distinct from 'heavy' dragoons. Sam Henry, an Irish journalist, wrote a column on ballads and broadsides from 1923–1939 in *The Northern Constitution* of Coleraine. The song 'Bonny light horseman', No 122 in the Sam Henry Collection, is in the Belfast Public Library. The first verse begins, 'When Boney commanded his armies for to stand | He levelled his cannons all over the land'. Henry says it was widely sung in the Napoleonic War period and remained in oral and broadside circulation for many years afterwards. As well as Cockney, Lord Worcester was fluent in the broad dialect of his native Gloucestershire.

3. Page 117: Sir Walter Scott mentions:

> a sister Lady Berwick who had whitewashed herself and cut Harriot. This was not to be forgiven and as both had boxes at the opera & Harriots [*sic*] was uppermost she had now and then an opportunity of revenging herself by spitting on her sisters [*sic*] head (letter to Lord Montagu, 18 February 1826).

4. Page 118: Gretna Green, on the Scottish border, where it was possible for minors to marry without parental consent.

5. Page 119: Lord Edward Somerset commanded the Household Brigade at Waterloo and had a narrow escape. His horse was killed and he had only just enough time to creep through a thick hedge and leap on to another horse before the enemy were upon him. Gronow writes:

> When Lord Uxbridge [formerly Lord Paget, later Marquis of Anglesea, first husband of the Duchess of Argyll] gave orders to Sir William Ponsonby and Lord Edward Somerset to charge the enemy, our cavalry advanced with the greatest bravery, cut through everything in their way, and gallantly attacked whole regiments of infantry; but eventually they came upon a masked battery of twenty guns, which carried death and destruction through our ranks, and our poor fellows were obliged to give way. The French cavalry followed on their retreat, when, perhaps, the severest hand-to-hand cavalry fighting took place within the memory of man. The Duke of Wellington was perfectly furious that this arm had been engaged without his orders, and lost not a moment in sending them to the rear, where they remained during the rest of the day. (*Reminiscences*, p74)

6. Page 119: Meyler's name appears with that of Brummell in Gronow's list of 'dandies ... who seemed to think that the principal object of their existence ought to be that of obtaining notoriety by their dress' ... The dandy costume was a blue coat with brass buttons, leather breeches, and top boots; 'and it was the fashion to wear a deep, stiff white cravat, which prevented you from seeing your boots while standing.' (*Reminiscences*, p57). In a well-known passage, Gronow describes the dandies – excepting Lord Alvanley, whom he liked – as:

> odious ... they arrogated to themselves the right of setting up their own fancied superiority on a self-raised pedestal, and despising their betters ... They hated everybody and abused everybody, and would sit together in White's bay window, or the pit boxes at the opera ... They swore a good deal, never laughed, had their own particular slang, looked hazy after dinner, and had most of them been patronised at one time or other by the Prince Regent (p167).

10

The 'Damned Sugar Baker'

Harriette consulted Sir John Boyd about Meyler. What was he like?

So beautiful and so sexy that women blushed when he looked at them, however respectfully, she was told. This news stimulated her.

'And whom does he love?'

'I understand his affections are currently divided among a Mrs Bang, a Mrs Patten and a Mrs Pancras, all ladies who haunt Covent Garden. He's a hard drinker, a hard rider, a good tennis player and cricketer; no fool, though he hates reading. Holds women very cheap and considers them mere instruments of pleasure, except for the Duchess of Beaufort – calls her a paragon.'

This description appealed to Harriette. It seemed piquant, a challenge after Worcester's sentimental adoration.

'Perhaps you'll show him to me some day at the opera?' she said.

The Duke of Beaufort sent a Mr Robinson – later a convicted fraudster – to demand the return of all Worcester's letters offering her marriage. Harriette asked for a week to decide and consulted a lawyer, who valued the letters at £20,000. Harriette reported this to Robinson, who said the Duke was expecting as much; Robinson advised Harriette that she might get even more by keeping the secrets of a noble family out of the courts. Harriette asked for time to consider and Robinson left frustrated.

Next morning the Duke and Duchess of Beaufort arrived in London with their son in tow. Worcester called on Harriette:

'My poor father is miserable and my mother is in hysterics because I refuse to go abroad without you.'

'Do you think they'd be happier if they had your promises to marry me in their hands?' she said.

'My father would do anything to get them, though they wouldn't do him any good, as I hope and intend to become your husband.'

Harriette, knowing how deeply in debt – and thus heavily dependent on his parents – Worcester was, wrote to the Duke pointing out that, far from pursuing his son, she had been pursued by him, and returning at the same time some of the letters. She delivered the packet herself to Grosvenor Square, but received no acknowledgement. The Duke returned to Badminton, taking Worcester with him. The young man managed to meet Harriette in London and near Brighton. He complained he was being bullied by family and friends, including Meyler, who pleaded respect for the Duchess as his motive.

Eventually a tear-soaked incoherent scrawl from Worcester announced that he had to go to Spain as Wellington's aide-de-camp; non-compliance would be interpreted as cowardice. He had, however, won permission to spend a last fortnight entirely with Harriette. Worcester begged her to travel with him, which she knew was impossible even had she wanted to. She burst into tears, realising belatedly that she had not given Worcester the gratitude he deserved. She was convinced that he would die in Spain while his regiment remained in England and it would all be her fault. Her best clothes, crimson velvet pelisse [coat] and white hat with feathers, were laid out ready for 'Hyde Park and conquests', while the poor boy's life was in danger. In floods of tears, she dressed and went to call on the Duke, who received her politely. She explained that, rather than send Worcester to his death, she would propose a separation, or even go abroad herself, to keep him out of danger.

The Duke told her it was folly and madness to think of marrying his son.

'You still imagine I want to force myself on your family and be despised? And do you imagine that if I wanted to marry your boy I wouldn't be able to?'

'I meant to say that such unequal marriages seldom or never succeed,' said the Duke.

'I am and always was determined not to marry him, and I've repeatedly told him so when he was on his knees imploring me to become his wife. I came in the hope that it would be unnecessary for Lord Worcester to join Wellington's staff. Goodbye. Will your Grace shake hands with me?'

The Duke frigidly complied.

Worcester came to London and spent every day with Harriette, despite urgent messages that the Duchess needed him on business, to which his answer was: 'Go to hell!' This was uncharacteristic, as he was usually polished and urbane. The plan was for Harriette to go with him to Spain, but it became clear to Harriette that this would not do, although a new maid had been hired and trunks packed. The army would not be stationary; if Harriette stayed in Lisbon she would see no more of him than she would if she were in London. She foresaw expense, misery, privation and insults if she became a camp-follower, and she was afraid of turning Worcester into a coward, unable to fight for worrying about her. The idea was abandoned. Worcester announced that he would agree to his father's demand of a year's absence but neither man nor devils would prevent his reunion with Harriette after that. He said mournfully, 'I'm leaving you, my beloved, in all the gaieties of London, surrounded by flatterers and my father's spies!'

'Never mind, my love,' said Harriette soothingly, 'if my living in London makes you miserable, I'll go and bury my wonderful charms in a village and make that village famous!'

'I have every confidence in your fidelity, and that's my only comfort,' moaned Worcester. Harriette tells us she was not in the least in love with him, but he was besotted with her. She treated him with 'friendly civility' so that the boy of twenty and the woman of twenty-six 'jogged on very well together':

> My mere friendship is … a match for many women's love … I always folded Worcester's neck handkerchiefs for him with my own hands, because he declared that nobody else understood them; and besides this, every Monday morning … read the housemaid a lecture about keeping his dressing room free from dust!

Worcester said he would not leave until his father agreed to pay Harriette an allowance while he was abroad. He brought Mr Robinson to her. Robinson explained that Worcester, being a minor, could sign no financial agreements himself that would stand up in law, but promised a quarterly sum from the Duke. Worcester was sure his father would honour this promise. Harriette, who claims to have been 'naturally careless in money matters', was reassured that she would not be left to starve.

Both shed tears on the day they parted.

'I'll write at least a quire of foolscap to you every day,' said Worcester, 'and may God bless my adored wife; I am ready to sacrifice my life for her happiness.' He had literally to be dragged away by Lord William Somerset. Otherwise, says Harriette, 'I almost believe he would have preferred love to glory and given old Wellington the slip.'

She passed a sleepless night, fretting that the gentle, loving lad had gone. Two days later, Robinson reappeared.

'Now be sensible,' he said. 'His Grace of Beaufort is willing to set you up in comfort for life; as I told you before, you can make your own terms, provided that you never speak or write to his lordship again.'

'Don't torment me like this when I'm so unhappy!' cried Harriette. 'You can tell the Duke from me that Worcester refused to leave England until I'd sworn to write to him often and to wait a year for him.'

Robinson went away in a bad temper, complaining that Harriette was impossible to do business with.

After Worcester had gone, Harriette's beloved sister Fanny was her constant visitor, doing everything she could to amuse and enliven her. Worcester had promised Fanny, on his own initiative, to get to know Colonel Parker in Spain and gather news of his doings. Fanny was still living with Julia, who was still adored by Mr Napier, almost young enough – and looking it – to be her son. Harriette's opera box had been paid for and Fanny and Julia had both bought tickets from her, but Harriette was disinclined to go without Worcester, the more so as his parents' box was opposite hers and she feared that visits from friends would be observed and misinterpreted, and then reported in such a way as to disturb poor Worcester's feelings. So, despite pressing entreaties from Julia, Harriette stayed at home.

A long letter arrived from Falmouth, where Worcester was waiting to leave England. To be still in the same country with his adored, beautiful wife, while knowing they could not meet again for a year, he wrote, was unbearable.

The following Saturday's opera was expected to be unusually brilliant. All the fashionable world was in town; there was a new ballet and a new French dancer, and Fanny said it was the height of folly to have paid two hundred guineas for an opera box without making use of it.

'Well,' said Harriette, 'Worcester can't get shot before he gets where he's going , can he? As soon as he's in any danger, I'll cut out all public amusements, but I might as well take the opportunity of seeing one or two more ballets.'

Amy had a box next to Harriette's. She was living with the Honourable Berkeley Paget[1], who had deserted his wife and family for her. Amy was taking her revenge on her rival – the Duchess of Argyll – by living with that rival's son from her first marriage. This caused a scandal; the Duke of York cut him dead and refused to receive him at Oatlands, on the grounds that 'a man ought to be of royal blood before he presumes to commit adultery, except in private'.

That evening, Harriette, Fanny and Julia were all elegantly dressed in new clothes. Men crowded around them, piqued at the possibility of replacing Worcester, whose entanglement with Harriette was now famous.

Brummell, Lord William Russell, Frederick Bentinck, Lord Molyneux, Captain FitzClarence, Lord Fife, the Duc de Berri, Lord Montagu and Berkeley Craven were among the visitors. A young man came up to Harriette and asked permission to present Mr Meyler, the rich young Hampshire gentleman who, according to Worcester, had spoken of Harriette so harshly. Fanny and Harriette were convinced he must be a spy set on to her by the Beauforts.

'Don't see him,' advised Fanny. 'I'm sure he'll make mischief.'

Harriette was intrigued by the description of Meyler's beauty and saw his professed dislike of her as a challenge. She thought he intended to seduce her and tell Worcester what a loose woman she was. He may not be aware, thought she, that I know him to be a friend of Worcester's family. So while the young man who had asked to present Meyler chatted to Julia, Harriette asked him what sort of person Meyler was. On hearing that he was a 'charming, beautiful youth' and that all the ladies were in love with him, she agreed to meet him[2]. He had an 'expressive countenance', writes Harriette. 'His manner too was particularly unaffected and gentlemanlike, and the tones of his voice were very sweet; nevertheless, it was easy to discover, in spite of his naturally good breeding, that he held me rather cheap.'

He promptly demonstrated this disrespect by attempting to kiss her as they went down the stairs of the theatre, 'but though I refused decidedly, it was done … on purpose that he might [be induced] to renew the attack at some future day, with a little more ceremony.' But, as Worcester's acknowleged mistress, she scorned to 'carry on a sly intercourse with another man' who disliked and despised her.

At three o'clock next day Harriette's servant announced a gentleman who refused to give his name, but said he lived in Grosvenor Square and wished to speak to her. She was about to insist on knowing his identity when she changed her mind. Her guess was right – the visitor was the Duke of Beaufort.

He was embarrassed. 'Harrumph,' he cleared his throat. 'Madam, the best thing — in short, it would be in your interest as well as my son's — you really should — er — abandon all hopes and cease corresponding with him, you know. Give up all that sort of thing, eh?'

'Duke,' interrupted Harriette, 'wasn't it your idea that Worcester should go abroad?'

'It was,' admitted the Duke.

'Well then,' said Harriette triumphantly, 'Lord Worcester positively and absolutely refused to leave London until I had solemnly promised to be faithfully his, and not place myself under the protection of any other man for twelve months after his leaving England. Are you asking me to break my word?'

The Duke was silent and stood against Harriette's door fidgeting and hesitating as though he wanted to say something important but lacked courage. There was a long pause. Then he blurted out, 'Who makes your shoes?'

Harriette stared in astonishment at this irrelevance.

' ... not to mention the feet and ankles ... ' mumbled His Grace.

This unexpected compliment took Harriette by surprise, so that she actually blushed and made polite enquiries about Worcester's health. His Grace left without saying much more.

Two more agonized, despairing letters came from Worcester at Falmouth, the second mailed the day before he sailed for Lisbon.

The next Saturday, Harriette in her usual white satin under white gauze, and wearing her diamond earrings, was sitting in her opera box when the thought of sexy young Meyler flashed into her mind. She wondered whether he would visit her box again. She half wanted him to, although she was indifferent to him; in addition, he had taken her availability for granted and said to other people that she was less than desirable. Deformed and ugly, was she? She'd show him!

Harriette to her sister Fanny: 'I should like to have just one more look at him before I die or retire to the country, if only to see if he's as beautiful as I remember.'

'You're very wicked to be thinking about him at all,' said Fanny.

'Meyler's face is even more delicious than darling Harry Mildmay's,' said Julia, 'and I must admit that if he were to approach me, I'd ditch Napier at once.'

That evening Meyler, sitting in the Duchess of Beaufort's box, did not acknowledge Harriette, Julia or Fanny. Harriette decided to be merry and live for the moment. Julia paid a visit to Amy's box and mentioned that Harriette thought Meyler very beautiful. Amy promptly despatched a common acquaintance to invite him to supper after the opera.

'Then I shan't go to Amy's,' said Harriette. 'I don't want to meet Meyler.' Meyler did not accept Amy's invitation. He was putting on a charade. Having tried a brash approach and been rebuffed, he pretended to the respect which Harriette demanded, confident he would eventually succeed. To him the pursuit was a game, the whim of a rich young man. Harriette did not notice how contradictory her feelings about him were. She implies she had her own home-made ethical code, but Julia's reading of her character as avid for money and for sexual adventure is more plausible. Harriette had moved to a house near where Julia and Fanny were living and spent a lot of time with them; she wrote long diary-letters to Worcester.

Next time Harriette went to the opera, she was visited by Lord Glengal, Luttrell, Nugent, Lord William Russell and others, all of whom enquired whether she had news of Worcester, and some of whom claimed to be in love with her. She tells us she remained faithful to Worcester, despite constant offers of protection. She was living on the Duke of Beaufort's modest allowance. Waiting while 'Fat' Nugent found her a cab, she noticed Meyler waiting as if on purpose to speak to her on the sly.

Harriette Wilson, she reflected, had refused to become Marchioness of Worcester to be waited for on a corner by a 'damned sugar baker'! She told Meyler she did not wish to know him.

'Why?' asked the young man.

'I consider you a dead bore,' she said, stepping into the carriage, followed by Julia. Fanny had left earlier with Colonel Parker. Nugent told the coachman to take them to Camden Town and wished them goodnight. They were scarcely clear of the throng of carriages when they saw a man in silk stockings running after them, bawling at the coachman to stop. It was Meyler, begging through the window to be allowed to come in for a few moments to apologize and explain. Harriette told him apologies and explanations were both superfluous.

'Mrs Johnstone,' appealed Meyler to Julia, 'please intercede for me. Do pray allow me to speak to you for five minutes. You may put me down again at White's in St James's Street, if you're tired of me.'

'Since there are two of us, it'll be all right,' said Julia – always with an eye to the proprieties – and, despite Harriette's protests, she pulled the check string and the carriage stopped. Meyler sat down next to Harriette and said he would be proud and happy to acknowledge her anywhere.

'I didn't mean to be rude,' said Harriette. 'I'm sorry, but you know how I stand with your friend Lord Worcester. I'm going to retire to Devonshire until he comes back, so there's no point in my making new friends.'

She was interrupted by a wail from Julia.

'What's the matter?' asked Harriette.

'I'm likely to be ruined! I had awful trouble getting two twenty-pound notes out of Napier at the opera tonight to settle a bill with and they're gone!' Julia scrabbled in her reticule in despair. They had reached Pall Mall. Meyler, glad to have something useful to do, asked them to wait in the coach while he ran back to search Harriette's box for the missing banknotes. Julia was frantic, as she was even more in debt than she dared to tell 'her stingy lover Napier'[3] and was – in Harriette's own words – 'pregnant as usual'[4] and feeling violently sick.

'What will become of me?' she moaned. 'I must go at once. I'd rather go to prison than let that charming young man see me vomit.'

'I can't keep you waiting in such a state,' said Harriette considerately. 'Set me down and drive off without me.'

'You can't wait in the street in evening dress,' protested Julia.

'I'll put my shawl over my head and give the watchman a shilling to take care of me; I won't miss Mr Meyler with your banknotes.'

Julia started to heave. Harriette insisted and Julia went.

In about ten minutes Meyler returned and seemed to be looking out for the cab.

'Here, Mr Meyler,' said Harriette, tapping him on the arm.

'No, no, not tonight,' said Meyler, pushing her away in the belief she was a woman of the streets.

'It's Harriette,' she said quietly. Astonished, he turned round.

'You here alone? Good heavens! I beg you ten thousand pardons!'

Harriette explained that Julia had been taken ill. Meyler at once propositioned Harriette, who refused him.

'I regret to say that no money was to be found; and unfortunately I've lent my own carriage to Lady Castlereagh this evening. How could I be so stupid! Let me at least find you another hackney coach.'

'Certainly not,' said Harriette. 'It's a warm, moonlit night, and I propose to walk home.' And in full evening dress they walked the couple of miles to Harriette's door, where they said goodnight and Meyler asked permission to call some day. He was pressing and Harriette finally said: 'You may call on me at Julia's next Thursday.' Having previously been rebuffed, he was delighted with this concession.

Next morning Harriette called on Julia.

'I've taken the liberty of inviting Meyler to your house because Lord Worcester would be miserable if I were to receive him in my own,' said Harriette.

Julia did not mind in the least. 'You know how much I admire that lovely creature Meyler. By the way, the banknotes were in my bosom all the while and

I want very much to apologize to that dear little man for all the trouble I've given him.'

Harriette was physically attracted to Meyler and she had not had sex recently. She blamed Julia for encouraging her to think of him, and reproached herself for disloyalty to Worcester. She wrote a brief note to Meyler excusing herself from 'meeting him at Mrs Johnstone's'. Julia told her that evening that Meyler had sat with her for more than two hours[5], hoping to see Harriette, and had gone away disappointed.

Next day Harriette received a letter from Meyler, begging permission to call. She did not reply and he 'took the liberty of coming to my house without permission'. Harriette's position, despite her bravado, was equivocal and insecure; she compensated, as we have seen, by insisting on punctilious formalities. He barged in past the servant and went upstairs to the sitting room, which Harriette had locked. As soon as the two women had succeeded in getting rid of him, Harriette sent him a note demanding 'a little more respect'. The following Saturday, Meyler visited the opera box which Harriette shared with Julia, so he could hardly be turned out. He took them home, but was not invited in, and Harriette refused to be alone with him. Julia chaperoned them as they walked in the fields then near Camden Town. Meyler was all sentimental adoration and flattery: Harriette says that he 'had so many little winning ways really they were overpowering to a poor weak woman! ... all these things and £30,000 a year[6] ... were enough to melt a heart of stone ... Meyler was so very humble, persevering and indefatigable, that he contrived to see and converse with me every day of my life in spite of all I could do to prevent him'. She never admitted him to her house or saw him alone. She wrote detailed letters about him to Worcester. She had small respect for Meyler, but his blatant sex appeal, combined with unremitting attention, disturbed her, and she told Worcester as much. To avoid temptation she proposed burying herself in Devonshire – easier said than done, as she knew herself. All the fashionable world seemed to find her attractive and delight in her conversation, and she was about to leave it all for a dull village, where she was to pass 'one of her most brilliant years' in solitude. Meyler offered her any terms she wanted to leave Worcester and live with him.

'You've said that fifty times already,' she said. 'I must follow the dictates of my own heart.' She was afraid that, if she left Worcester for Meyler, Worcester would challenge his rival to a duel and one of them or both might be killed. She told Meyler she was half in love with him and that she had never been in love with Worcester. Meyler said he would wait the full year and made extravagant promises, which Harriette laughed at. Meanwhile Worcester continued to pour out his heart in romantically tender, interminable letters, with excellent descriptions of battles and a long account of Colonel Parker, for Fanny. It was these kind letters that finally decided Harriette to leave London[7].

Notes to Chapter Ten

1. Page 125: The Honourable Berkeley Paget (1780–1842) was sixth son of Henry, Lord Paget, first Earl of Uxbridge, later Marquis of Anglesey. His mother married the Duke of Argyll.

2. Page 125: According to Julia, Harriette met Meyler ('an accomplished rake with a large fortune and little prudence') at Amy's (*Confessions*, p223)

3. Page 128: Harriette stigmatizes several men as 'stingy' without specifying what they got for their money. It is not hard to guess.

4. Page 128: Harriette clearly knew something the perpetually pregnant Julia did not. Julia claims that Harriette pretended pregnancy in order to snare Worcester, but at Charmouth became actually pregnant (*Confessions*, p238). See Chapter 11.

5. Page 129: Two hours was a long time; the normal length of a social call was fifteen to thirty minutes.

6. Page 129: Jane Austen's wealthiest fictional character, Mr Rushworth in *Mansfield Park* (1814), has £12,000 a year; in real life Meyler, at the same time, had, according to the highest estimate, nearly three times as much.

7. Page 130: Harriette wrote bitterly in 1825:

> … being now in the daily habit of meeting this profligate Marquis of Worcester about Paris, with the sister of his late wife, and seeing him look as if he did not even know me by sight, while I often forget, until he has passed, where or when I have seen that man before, the face being familiar, and, perhaps, the name even forgotten – 'Oh, by-the-bye!' I say to myself, if I meet him a second time in the same morning, 'now I think of it, that long-nosed tall man is Worcester.' And just in this way does his own treacherous memory no doubt treat his own 'dearest dear; own beloved! ever adored, and ever to be adored! delicious! sweet! darling! wife! Harriette.'

11

STORMY WEATHER

Quixotically Harriette decided she owed Worcester this sacrifice. She asked
Luttrell about villages and he suggested Charmouth, within thirty miles of
Exeter. She booked seats for herself and her maid on the Exeter mail coach at
once. Meyler was 'half-cooled' by this decision, but it saddened him
nevertheless; he asked permission to write to her. She agreed, but insisted that
all letters must be shown to Worcester. However, she promised that if she ever
left Worcester: 'I will gladly come to you.'

'In a year, then,' said Meyler, 'if Worcester does not return?'

Harriette replied that everything depended on circumstances.

Meyler shed a tear when they parted and gave Harriette a gold toothpick
case with some of his hair in it. Harriette soon regretted her impulsive removal[1];
she and her maid were quickly bored. She gives us a delightful vignette,
however, of Lyme Regis:

> … a sort of Brighton in miniature, all bustle and confusion, assembly
> rooms, donkey-riding, raffling, etc. It was sixpence per night to attend
> the assemblies, and much cheaper if paid by the season. We went to a
> little inn and dined. From the window, I was much amused to see the
> number of smart old maids … tripping down the streets, in turbans or
> artificial flowers twined round their wigs, on the light fantastic toe, to
> the sixpenny tea-rooms at five in the evening … as we walked past their
> windows we saw them all drinking tea and playing cards. There were
> amongst them persons of the highest rank; but the society was chiefly
> composed of people of very small independent fortunes, who for
> economy had settled at Lyme Regis …

The landlady at the inn told Harriette that it would be difficult to find lodgings
in Charmouth. Eventually she found a naval widow, with a daughter who took
a fancy to Harriette, who invited her to share their home without making
enquiries. Harriette decided to act with the strictest propriety, to 'set an
example' by going regularly to church, and concluded she was under no
obligation to 'turn king's evidence' against herself by drawing attention to what
the genteel Miss Eliza Higgins had called her 'little peccadilloes'. Her hosts
charged too little and showed her every kindness.

Julia writes that she accompanied Harriette to Charmouth – Harriette taking up with a Mr Roche on the way and 'sleeping with him at every stage' of the three-day journey. Julia says that Harriette had a baby at Charmouth by a married Lieutenant Devall, which was put out to nurse. Julia writes:

> Once she nearly betrayed her *calling* in the country, as we were going to church, by holding up her leg on passing a stile and desiring the clergyman to fasten her bootlace. He had been once a dasher in the London streets and very gallantly complied with her request, saying with a smile: 'Don't your garter want tightening, my love?' I could have brained her with my fan[2].

Soon, though, Harriette was fretting for a letter from Meyler. One arrived from Worcester full of vows of eternal love, describing a battle won and saying he could already speak Spanish. Harriette says he had always had a remarkable memory, and adds patronisingly that he could have been a clever man if he had only had the habit of reflection. There was also a letter from Meyler, who claimed to be unwell and in need of country air. He was often depressed and habitually complained of feeling poorly until he had downed a few bottles of claret. She wrote back that she hoped he would be kind and honourable enough not to intrude on her in Devon: 'How you would laugh to see me in my quiet straw bonnet, trotting down the hill to church, and lending my arm to the curate's father, aged ninety-five ... '

Meyler took the hint and did not come, but wrote constantly. He was soon elected Member of Parliament for Winchester, which cost him £20,000. He told Harriette in a letter: 'I had not the smallest idea that it was necessary to kiss so many dirty, ugly women, and drink so much ale, rum and milk, grog, raisin and elder wine, with porter and cider, all in one day ... I have been sick for a fortnight ... ' Worcester continued to write sweet nothings at inordinate length. When she wrote her *Memoirs*, Harriette wryly recalled these passionate effusions and apostrophised him as 'now a cold-blooded profligate':

> Poor Worcey! You ought to have seen me provided for, and yet I can never quite forget how dearly you loved me, when you gave up all society, endured almost a parent's curse; nay, more, gave up hunting and offered to support me by driving a mail coach!

Meanwhile, the Duke of Beaufort had discontinued the quarterly payments on which Harriette depended. She was in debt for her board and lodging. She wrote to an attorney called Fisher, seeking legal advice, but he imagined she was after an assignation, so refused to see her. She wrote to Meyler complaining that his friends, the Beauforts, were treating her badly. She waited another month and then wrote to the Duke, threatening to join Lord Worcester in Spain. A remittance arrived by the next post, accompanied by a letter saying the fault was Mr Robinson's.

Worcester was unable to return at the end of the year, as the Prince Regent had been persuaded by the wily Duke of Beaufort to order the Prince's Own Regiment, the 10th Hussars, abroad. Worcester wrote heartbroken letters and Harriette planned to leave for Spain, though she would have preferred to go back to London. She was waiting at Falmouth for a fair wind, when she heard that Worcester had run away with a Mrs Archdeacon, sister of the second wife of a paymaster in the 10th.

What a fool, she thought. After tormenting his parents and burying me down here, suddenly to take another woman away, despite his last letter full of solemn declarations of undying love! What steadiness could I expect from such an ass[3]? She decided to go back to London and have some fun with Meyler. Her determination was increased on hearing a rumour that, if Harriette Wilson tried to join Lord Worcester, the English ambassador had been authorized to put her on a ship and send her to America. She never found out whether or not this was true, but Worcester did not write, and was said by everybody to be living with another woman. Harriette went to Fanny's house in London. Meyler was in the country and Harriette proposed writing to him.

Fanny was horrified. 'For heaven's sake, get the Duke of Beaufort to do something for you first!' she cried, and repeatedly made the same point. Harriette wrote to the Duke saying she was now ready to put herself under Meyler's protection, as soon as the Duke provided for her at the rate of £500 a year. The Duke wrote back denying he had ever offered so much, and stuck at £300: 'More than that I must decline,' he added. Harriette agreed, and the Duke set his attorney to work to draw up the papers. Two large letter-parcels arrived unexpectedly from Worcester. He indignantly denied seducing Mrs Archdeacon – Mrs Archdeacon had followed him and he had sent her packing immediately; he wished her dead and only thought of his adored Harriette, he said. Harriette wrote to the Duke saying that circumstances had changed and she was not going to Meyler after all. Shortly afterwards, the Duke heard of Mrs Archdeacon and, rubbing his hands together in the belief that Harriette was rejected by Worcester, wrote to Harriette saying that she could starve for all he cared. Harriette replied that she still had letters from Worcester promising marriage. Rattled, the Duke retorted that if she proved humble and grateful, he might be persuaded to offer a small sum for the letters, but warned her not to be too greedy.

Enraged, Harriette threatened to publish Worcester's promises unless the Duke gave her £300 a year. The Duke was sufficiently panicked to offer her an annuity of £200, on condition that she never spoke or wrote to Worcester again. Harriette gave up the letters to the Duke, who wrote to his son in Spain, and documents were drawn up. Worcester poured out his heart in letters to Fanny and eventually to Harriette herself. Harriette impulsively wrote to Worcester, breaking the terms of her agreement with his father, who cancelled the annuity and demanded the first £100 back.

'For this I had left the gay world and buried myself in a village,' writes Harriette. She had hoped to earn the gratitude and respect of Worcester's parents by refusing to marry the infatuated boy – and this was her reward. Despondently she wrote to her other admirer, Mr Meyler, accusing Worcester of being in the plot to take away her hush-money. In her final paragraph she said: 'The money is nothing … but all this harsh treatment wounds me more than I can describe … ' Harriette received £1,200 down in settlement of the affair. Her legal adviser was Henry Peter Brougham (1778–1868), later first Viscount Brougham, who was to defend George IV's Queen Caroline at her trial for adultery in 1820[4]. Harriette paid Brougham in kind.

Meyler replied that he was coming to London at once. He had believed her to be in Spain with Worcester: 'Never mind Worcester's annuity,' he wrote grandly, 'for you and I shall never part … ' He promised never to marry 'any woman on earth'.

When they met, Harriette was overwhelmed by his manly beauty. Worcester had never engaged either her heart or her senses; now her pulses throbbed again. They took a good house in the New Road, close to Gloucester Place. For the first fortnight they were both in love and did not quarrel, but by the third week Harriette had found out that Meyler had a foul temper. After being pampered and indulged by the besotted Worcester, Harriette found Meyler's violent, unpredictable rages hard to bear, although they were followed by passionate lovemaking. She neither respected nor trusted him, yet she was sexually enthralled and deeply jealous. She tells us his expression was of such voluptuous beauty that he was irresistible.

One evening, when she saw him sitting in the Duchess of Beaufort's box, Harriette left her own[5] and sent a message asking him to come out in order to speak to a person in the passage. When he appeared, she threatened to leave him if he ever went back to the Duchess's box. Meyler was flattered, knowing that she had never been possessive about Worcester. When they got home, he asked her why she agitated herself about nothing.

'You know how fond you have been of the Duchess,' sulked Harriette. 'You were in love with her.'

Meyler denied it. He explained that he and Worcester had been at Christ Church together. 'One day, when I was too young to have had intrigues except with street women in Oxford, he introduced me to his mother. As you know, she's still good-looking, an attractive woman. I felt a strong desire for her, but without the faintest hope, although she paid me unusual attention. One night, when I was staying at Badminton while the Duke was away, I complained that my lips were chapped and sore. It was midnight and the Duchess said to me,

"Come to my dressing room; I'll give you some cold cream." When I went in, her night-clothes were hanging to air near the fire. We were alone. I hesitated. In another minute, I might have ventured to take this midnight invitation as a hint, but unfortunately Lady Harrowby, who probably suspected something improper, came into the room at that moment.'

Meyler and Harriette lived a stormy life, assuaged by sexual passion. Their lovemaking was violent, with bruises, bites and scratches. He grudged her visits to the opera and frequently left her alone in order to stay with the Beauforts at Badminton, which reduced her to misery[6]. He told her he would rather blow his brains out than be the slave of any woman. His, he said, was not the passion of a day, or even of a year: 'I shall never stop loving you,' said Meyler, striking his head with his hand, 'but I must have some freedom.'

Harriette listened to what he said. She hoped Meyler's volatile passion was more durable than Worcester's lachrymose rapture, now a burst balloon. Meyler, rolling rich, handsome, and exciting in bed, was worth hanging on to. I'll put up with him as long as he's faithful, she decided, aware than many rivals wished themselves in her shoes.

Next day Meyler dined with Harriette, intending to set off for Badminton. Harriette proudly held back her tears, played his favourite tunes on the pianoforte and cheerfully drank champagne. He picked at his food and only sipped his wine.

'What's the matter?' she asked. He sighed.

'If you loved me, you wouldn't be so cheerful, knowing as you do that I'm about to visit an attractive woman,' sulked Meyler.

'Nonsense!' cried Harriette. 'You promise never to leave me, and I believe you; a jealous, nagging woman is contemptible; so let's enjoy time present.'

'You're delighted to get rid of me, I can see,' said Meyler. 'I can't believe any woman can love me without being jealous. I'm going to punish you by not going to Badminton after all.'

Harriette kissed him. 'Good! So you'll stay with me, then? I'm so happy. I was only pretending not to mind.'

Satisfied it would make her miserable, Meyler spitefully set off for Badminton the next morning. That evening, Harriette went to her sister Amy's, where among others she met Lord Yarmouth.

Harriette, tiring by this time of Meyler's tantrums, asked Lord Yarmouth whether it was possible to spend one's life with a bad-tempered man.

'Better live on a bone,' answered his lordship, his mouth full of cold partridge.

Harriette laughed at him: 'What would you know about living on a bone?'

Fanny urged Harriette to leave Meyler at once: 'His jealousy is only selfishness. He goes to balls and parties and never goes home till five or six in the morning, yet he always calls here to ask why you aren't at home in bed.'

'Red Herrings', Lord Yarmouth, later Marquis of Hertford

Everybody advised Harriette to cut loose, and somebody mentioned Worcester. Fanny had heard from him that morning. He had heard that Harriette was living with Meyler in a house she had once shared with him. He declared that he himself could never live in it with any other woman. Harriette was disgusted with him and with the entire Beaufort family; she could not forgive Worcester for showing his father the letter he had slily coaxed from her, causing her to lose her annuity.

Lord Yarmouth whispered: 'You really must pay me a visit at my little private door in Park Lane tomorrow. You know you can rely on my discretion.

The King dines with me; but His Majesty will leave me before the play is over, and I'll open the door for you myself after my people have gone to bed. You'll find everything ready and comfortable.'

Harriette agreed to go. The next evening she was with Fanny and Julia in a box at Covent Garden by seven o'clock. As the curtain dropped, Harriette said to them: 'Are you hungry?'

'Very,' they replied together. They had dined early and sat through a long play.

'Well, we live in the age of fairies!' said Harriette playfully. 'You'll see! A kind fairy is going to tap on a door with her wand and it'll fly open, and you'll see a magnificent repast, served on gold and silver … '

'Stop it,' pleaded Fanny. 'I'll be lucky if my maid has saved us a bone of mutton or half a pint of beer. Times are hard.'

'What would you say I was if I'd discovered a fairy – would you call me a witch? Or a magician?'

Fanny and Julia were unconvinced, but Harriette persuaded them to be led by her. Some years previously they had been shown Lord Yarmouth's private apartments via a secret passage, but had never been through the little entrance in Park Lane. The cab set them down some distance from it and the night was dark. Harriette was feeling her way.

'Where on earth are you taking us?' cried Julia, alarmed. 'There are no houses here; this place is really dangerous. Let's go back to the carriage.'

Harriette soothed her and promised that in half a minute they would see what the good fairy had provided. Reaching the little low door, like the entrance to a cellar, she tapped gently three times. The door was opened by Lord Yarmouth, astonished to see three ladies when he expected only one. However, good manners concealed his disappointment, and he turned the incident into a joke. The visitors went up a little winding staircase to his beautiful rooms, where they enjoyed a lavish meal, staying till three in the morning.[7]

Meyler came back early to town, fearful that Harriette might be unfaithful. He began picking quarrels. He was offended if she was seen with her sisters at the opera, though he met his own friends there. He was a close friend of Sir Harry Mildmay, Julia's faithless lover. Harry enjoyed poaching other men's wives and mistresses, and caused much mischief. He mocked Meyler for staying with Harriette 'like a shepherd', and urged him to take up with 'women of fashion'.

One evening after the opera he teased Harriette with a story of seeing Meyler get into a coach with another woman. It was a rainy night and Fanny and Julia were going in Napier's coach in a different direction from Harriette's. Mildmay offered Harriette a lift to the house in New Road she shared with Meyler, but took her instead to his own house in Brook Street. He took her hand and tried to pull her indoors.

'I shall walk home,' she cried, 'or at least until I find a coach; and I insist on your leaving me this instant.'

He ignored her command and in his turn insisted on walking her home. The rain had stopped. Harriette was afraid that Meyler would turn violent and hoped that, if he did, Sir Harry would protect her.

'If Meyler isn't there, I'll come in,' said shameless Sir Harry.

'What do you think he'd say if he found you in his house?' asked Harriette, astonished.

'Oh, hang Meyler! We'd lock him out.'

Such cheek made Harriette laugh, though she was afraid of Meyler's rage.

The servant was coming down the garden to open the gate. Harriette asked if Meyler was in, and learned he had gone to Amy's to look for her. Harriette told the servant to shut the door and begged Sir Harry to go away, as she could not afford to be seen with him. He refused.

'I didn't really see him leave after the opera, you know! It was just a trick to get you to myself!' he said. 'I left him in the upper room talking to Lord Palmerston.'

'He'll kill me!' said Harriette. A couple of drunks, imagining Harriette to be a street-walker, started catcalling and knocking with their sticks on the iron railings. Sir Harry ran after them and Harriette knocked on her own door, was let in, and Sir Harry was shut out.

Half an hour later, Meyler's carriage turned up at the door. It was three o'clock in the morning. Harriette was terrified. To her surprise, he was calm. He took both her hands, kissed them and gazed into her eyes.

'You'll not deceive me,' he said. 'I'm certain of that.'

'I've nothing to hide,' said Harriette. 'I've done nothing wrong.'

Meyler, having been told by Amy that Harriette had left in Sir Harry's carriage, had looked for Julia and Fanny to ask where Harriette was, but they had gone with Napier.

'I drove at once to Julia's, but nobody there had any idea where you were, and Napier mocked me, so that I hid my anxiety for fear of looking a total fool, but everybody saw through me. I left them to go to Amy's. She said everything she could to convince me you were with Mildmay. I came here to check before I called on him.'

Harriette told Meyler how Sir Harry had lied to her.

'I shan't be angry with him so long as you refuse him,' said Meyler. 'I've been wanting some such story to tease him with, because he tells so many about me.'

Stimulated by jealousy, Meyler made violent love to Harriette with more excitement than ever. At this time, he lived separately in Grosvenor Square, but paid Harriette's rent. He was summoned by Lord Palmerston, then secretary-at-war to the Tory government, to regimental duties, and acquired a uniform. He replied to the summons that he was due in the House of Commons to oppose a bill for Catholic emancipation[8].

Meyler, who stuck to the older fashion of silk stockings, cotton breeches and knee-buckles, was quiet and anything but military in his manner. His hands were fashionably small, white and soft. One night at the opera Fanny said to Harriette: 'Do you know Lord Worcester is expected to bring home the next despatches?'

'It's all the same to me since he was mean enough to tell his father I'd written to him,' said Harriette. 'I'll never like him nor respect him again.'

'I had a letter from him this morning,' said Fanny. 'He writes tenderly about you and about how a friend of his saw you in Hyde Park, looking lovely. He said he'd love to see you[9] –'

'Never mind Worcester,' interrupted Harriette, 'I can't imagine why Meyler isn't visiting us this evening.' She kept an eye on the Duchess of Beaufort's box, but he wasn't there either. Harriette went down the grand staircase after the show, feeling neglected and cross. A voice called her from a little dark corner: it was Meyler, in full regimentals. Fanny and Harriette laughed at him; Julia asked him why, having dressed up, he was hiding.

'I'm going to the Duke of Devonshire's dress ball, where I expect to see plenty of other fools in this ridiculous costume. I can't face people looking like this. I've been stuck here for two hours trying to get to your box, but I'm too embarrassed to go to my own carriage till everybody has gone.'

He looked so handsome in his red coat with yellow facings that Harriette was struck with jealousy. She tried to persuade him not to go. He said he must, but she could go back to her house in his carriage.

'Are you going back to your house in Grosvenor Square first?'

'Yes.'

On the way to her own home Harriette could not bear being excluded by her role from the gaieties of society, as she had been ever since her liaison with Fred Lamb. Impulsively she pulled the check-string and asked to be driven to Meyler's house. Unannounced, she walked up to his dressing room.

'Meyler,' she said, 'I've always given way to your whims. This time, please indulge mine for once. I'm feeling low, mentally and physically, tonight. Please cut the Duke and come back with me. I've never interfered with your pleasures before, so please don't refuse me.'

He was obstinate, but finally took off his uniform and went home with her.

Soon afterwards Meyler went hunting at Melton Mowbray in Leicestershire[10], where Harriette was not welcome, but Harriette took post-horses and joined him as a surprise. He seemed delighted to see her and invited her to dine at their club. She found life in Leicestershire, however, disappointingly dull. The men were off after foxes at six in the morning, dressed up in old single-breasted coats that had once been red, and came back to dinner at six. Their hunt evening dress was red and white and most becoming to handsome young men. While they sat at table, a handful of squalid prostitutes would come and tap on their windows. Those men not too sleepy would sneak out of the room. The rest snored and drank till ten and went to bed till hunting time again.

When the signal of what Harriette calls 'those horrible, dirty prostitutes' was slyly answered by Mildmay, Lord Herbert and Berkeley Craven, handsome and elegant, Harriette thought it a great shame. In one of his rages Meyler said she was such a loose woman that he was afraid to leave the room in case she offered herself as an indoor substitute for the dirty, shivering ones outside. Harriette indignantly repudiated the notion. But she confesses frankly to us that she thought of it.

'I forget,' writes Harriette airily, 'whether Meyler got tired of me, or I of Melton, or of him; … but I very soon returned to town.'

Notes to Chapter Eleven

1. Page 131: 'Her passions were as an impetuous torrent,' writes Julia (*Confessions*, p232).

2. Page 132: *Confessions*, p229.

3. Page 133: Worcester distinguished himself by gallantry in Spain and in 1835 succeeded his father as seventh Duke of Beaufort. They were reconciled on the father's deathbed. The son became Member of Parliament for West Gloucestershire, Master of the Beaufort Hounds and a great patron of field sports in general, living mainly on his estate. His dinners at Badminton when he became Duke were exquisite, and his claret cup a famous 'nectar'. Soon after parting from Harriette, he made a suitable marriage with Georgiana Frederica Fitzroy, the Duke of Wellington's niece. However, Worcester seems to have been seriously lacking in sexual confidence and to have been indeed the 'ass' Harriette said he was.

Mrs Arbuthnot suggests that his marriage was unhappy:

> Lady Worcester died after a week's illness of inflammation brought on by going into a cold bath after dancing at the ball at Carlton House. She was only twenty-eight, one of the handsomest women in England, had made the most brilliant marriage and was flattered, followed and admired by all the world. It is sad to contrast all this brilliancy with the cold and dreary grave ... and yet she will then have more tranquillity, for her prospects were not happy ones. Lord Worcester, overwhelmed with debts, had lately had executions in his house and, if the Duke of Wellington had not given her rooms in his house, she would not have had a hole to put her head into. He was inconstant, too, and she, vain and fond of admiration, might not always have avoided the temptations which surrounded her ... (*Diary* , 11 May, 1821).

The previous year there had been gossip about Lady Worcester and Francis Russell. Mrs Arbuthnot grieved for the two small daughters left 'to the care of a father so inconsiderate and light-minded'. Light-minded he certainly was. Six months later, Mrs Arbuthnot recorded that Lord Worcester was engaged to Lady Jane Paget, second daughter of Lord Anglesey by his first wife (she who after her divorce had become Duchess of Argyll):

> ... the day after Lady Worcester was buried ... he went to the Isle of Wight where he found Lady Jane and the whole thing was settled between them in less than *ten days*! ... The Duke seems much disgusted ... but he says he is the most extraordinary person about women ... while he was ... writing every day to Lady Jane, he was flirting violently with Lady Mildmay [Sir Harry's second wife], making desperate love to a French girl who lived with her, and had besides affairs going on with two or three girls at the Opera' (4 November 1821).

Four months after this entry, Worcester was generally believed to be in love with his late wife's half-sister, Emily Frances Smith, despite writing passionate letters to Lady Jane and signing himself 'your affectionate husband', which gave rise to well-founded accusations that he was 'unsteady'. The Duchess of Beaufort, writes Mrs Arbuthnot, 'has been much annoyed about it' (7 February 1822). In March Worcester broke off his engagement to Lady Jane, by writing to her father, Lord Anglesey. Lady Jane was distressed but her father wisely said she was lucky to have escaped. By June, the Duke of Wellington was also annoyed, as Emily was the daughter of Wellington's sister by her second marriage. Worcester, his wife thirteen months dead, was consulting lawyers about marrying Emily, as it was forbidden to marry a deceased wife's sister. Wellington tried to persuade Worcester to go abroad, and visited Emily's father, advising him to lock her up and make sure she was not alone with Lord Worcester till it had been decided whether or not such a marriage was valid. However Mr Smith, was 'such a fool and managed so ill that at night she went out of the house to join him and they left town together'. The marriage, of dubious legality, took place on June 29 1822. On 2 July Lord Alvanley received a letter from Lord Worcester making enquiries about a Miss Coleman, with whom he had been flirting; it was this flirtation which had made Miss Smith - who was far from pretty, with a long, thin, projecting nose - so anxious to secure him.

4. Page 134: Brougham (1778-1868) was later Lord Chancellor under a Whig government. He was co-founder with Sydney Smith and Francis Jeffrey of the *Edinburgh Review*, which attacked Byron. Brougham was in 1825 a founder of London University, helped to pass the 1832 Reform Bill and supported the abolition of slavery. He made Cannes a smart resort.

5. Page 134: Harriette may be stretching the truth at this point, since - according to Julia - the box had been given up as too expensive (*Confessions*, p317).

6. Page 135: Repeating the story of the Duchess of Beaufort, Meyler and the cold cream, was Harriette's revenge on the family who had, she believed, injured her. The Duchess was a religious woman.

7. Page 137: Julia says she never visited Lord Yarmouth by a secret door in her life (*Confessions*, p271). However, Lord Yarmouth had a reputation for debauchery; possibly the evening did not end so innocently as Harriette suggests: Lord Yarmouth, after all, found his lubricious wishes answered in triplicate. It is possible that an orgy took place, from which Julia was anxious to dissociate herself.

8. Page 139: Discriminatory laws against Roman Catholics were not abolished until the Catholic Emancipation Act of 1829.

9. Page 139: The Beauforts and their relatives were still terrified. Lady Bessborough wrote to Worcester's uncle by marriage, Lord Granville Leveson-Gower - he who had been marched about London on a hot summer day - :

Apropos of throwing away happiness, I must tell you another part of Lady Melbourne's letter, which concerns you more nearly. She was told that Harriette Wilson is living at Ryde in great retirement, passing for the most Virtuous Woman in the Island; and that she is waiting for Lord W's coming of age, when he is to return and marry her. She shows some of his letters, all ending with 'yr. affec. Husband' (24 September 1812).

10. Page 139: In *Pelham* the affected Mr Ritson says ' ... I only hunt in Leicestershire ... 'tis not the thing to hunt anywhere else' (Chapter 40).

12

A Shock for Fanny

It was 1814. Napoleon was on Elba and it seemed the war was over. The Emperor of Russia and the King of Prussia were in London that June to consolidate the alliance against Napoleon[1] and three royal heads were to be seen in one box at the opera, for the Prince Regent, later George IV, was with them. Tickets were sold for thirty guineas, then a huge sum.[1]

There was a grand masquerade at Wattier's Club, for all the nobility of England, to celebrate the peace between England and France. Wattier's was famous for good food and high play; whole fortunes were lost there at faro, macao and hazard. Until 1819, when it fell into disrepute as a haunt of swindlers, Wattier's was extremely fashionable. Amy, Fanny and Harriette all managed to wangle tickets; Julia's applications to members of the club who were stewards of the feast all proved unsuccessful, until she approached Lord Yarmouth.

'I'm not a member,' he said, 'so I can't get you a lady's ticket, but if you fancy going in boy's clothes, I have one to spare – not transferable, mind.'

Julia was very shy and the idea embarrassed her, but her legs were beautiful, and she was persuaded to show them in black satin knee-breeches. Harriette went with her to Mr Stultz[2], the German regimental tailor and moneylender in Clifford Street. Julia wore sheer silk stockings, black satin shoes with large red rosettes, a French cambric shirt with finely-pleated sleeves, a sleeveless blue silk jacket trimmed with silver buttons, and a plain black hat with a red silk band and bow.

As Julia's girl-friend, Harriette wore a red silk skirt with a high-waisted black satin jacket, trimmed with buttons that matched Julia's. Her shoes were red leather and black satin, her silk stockings blue with small red clocks. Her small hat was pea-green and saucily perched on one side at the back of her head, over a profusion of 'careless' ringlets. Fanny dressed as a country housemaid, wearing short sleeves to show her lovely arms. Amy went, to Harriette's amusement, as a nun. She still lived with Berkeley Paget and went everywhere with him in public, especially to the opera, where the real Mrs Berkeley Paget frequently went herself. Harriette considered such lack of discretion thoroughly vulgar.

The expected crowd was enormous and the party were advised to get into their carriage at five in the hope of arriving between nine and ten. The journey of a couple of miles took four hours. Guests were welcomed by the Dukes of Devonshire and Leinster, who were in the uniform of club members for the evening: light blue dominoes [loose cloaks], without masks. Every lady was presented with a free raffle ticket; prizes ranged in value from a guinea to twenty-five guineas; there were souvenir bracelets, watches, lockets, boxes, all bearing images of Wellington, now made a Duke. The club was like a fairy palace, with a beautiful conservatory. Curtains of green satin matched the ottomans, fringed with silver. In various rooms there were performances by the famous clown Grimaldi, rope dancers, jugglers, singers and ballet dancers.

A person dressed as an old, grand maiden lady of Queen Anne's day, her face patched and painted, was Colonel Armstrong. He sat on a bench, with his hoops and ruffles and high powdered wig, fanning himself and chatting to his young maids of honour, actually young men, also in period costumes. Considering his unilateral decision to give up sexual relations with his young partner, Lucy, this emasculating choice of costume seems significant. Passing friends kept up the charade, pretending not to recognize him. People puzzled over Julia: was she a real boy or a girl?

Supper was served at half-past one and dancing went on till seven next morning. The wines were delectable and club members waited on their guests, most of whom were wearing masks as well as fancy dress. Harriette, wandering in an empty room, was addressed by a masked stranger in a rich Spanish costume of white satin and ostrich feathers in his hat, who kissed her passionately, said he had always adored and watched over her, adding that it was he who anonymously sent her banknotes. Harriette enjoyed the kisses and hoped the stranger might be Ponsonby, but he abruptly left her. Had it been Ponsonby, she would surely have recognized the voice. Meyler spent a long time finding Harriette, who had been chatting to Lord Byron[3,] and when he found her refused to leave her side, his fancy for the moment rekindled.

Harriette's father was intending to abandon her unhappy, brow-beaten mother, and return to his native Switzerland. He hoped his wife and younger children would move to France, where living was cheaper, an arrangement Lord Berwick thoroughly approved of; the Baron preferred his embarrassing in-laws to be at a distance across the Channel.

Worcester came back to England for a fortnight and made up to various ladies, including the Duke of Wellington's niece, Georgiana Frederica Fitzroy, whom he was to marry later that year. He visited Fanny, who tried to coax him into doing something for Harriette, but she found him changed from a shy, sensitive, blushing boy into a cold-blooded sensualist. Harriette still hankered after Meyler's kisses, although they pretended not to see each other at the opera and in the round room where people socialised afterwards. They made it up, agreeing that they would not live together, but he would visit. Harriette decided to go to Paris and establish herself in lodgings and Meyler proposed to follow her. He had been consoling himself in Leicestershire with a woman who called herself Mrs Stonyer because she lived with a Mr Stonyer.

He confessed to Harriette how the affair was managed: 'We all go out hunting together and after a few miles I wink at the others and fall off my horse or pretend to have hurt my ankle. I then say how annoying it is to have to go home. Stonyer offers to come with me but I insist he mustn't lose his day's sport, and I go back to his mistress.' However, when Mrs Stonyer grew jealous and possessive, the fickle Meyler lost interest in this indoor sport.

Harriette was taken up, on one of her visits to France, by a Mrs Nesbit, a relative of Lord Bathurst. Harriette was enjoying the company of some agreeable young men when Mrs Nesbit drew her into a cold and dirty bedroom, and insisted on displaying huge red boils that made it agony for her to sit down. Harriette was disgusted and to get rid of her said at dinner, 'I'm puzzled how, with such a strong sense of propriety, you came to show me, an utter stranger, your bum-fiddle.'

'This,' said Mrs Nesbit, rising to leave the room with a reserved and dignified air, 'shall be a lesson to me against forming hasty friendships.'

'Or showing your bum-fiddle,' said Harriette, laughing.

Colonel Parker, Fanny's lover, returned from Spain without telling Fanny. Hearing he was in an hotel in Vere Street, Fanny set off on foot, hoping it could not be true, but greatly agitated in case it was. She met him on the hotel steps and, breathless and speechless, put her hand on his arm.

'Fanny,' he said, 'you are no doubt surprised that I didn't come to you or tell you I was in town, but … ' He paused.

'Pray, speak,' said Fanny, pressing both hands to her left side, where she suffered intermittent pain. She could scarcely breathe and her trembling lips were blue.

'I have bad news for you,' said Parker awkwardly. He paused before blurting out: 'I'm going to be married.'

Fanny collapsed and Parker called a cab and took her home to Julia's, where she and Harriette were sitting. Fanny had furnished a back parlour as her sitting room, overlooking the garden. Julia and Harriette expected Parker and Fanny to join them in the drawing room, but they did not come up. When dinner was on the table, the servant knocked on Fanny's door and told Colonel and 'Mrs' Parker that the others were waiting. They refused to come to the meal. Harriette, concerned for her favourite sister, simply went in without knocking. Fanny was sitting on the sofa, gazing at the floor, without tears, but her face was swollen. Harriette was frightened for her.

'My dearest Fanny, what's the matter?'

Fanny made no response.

'Colonel Parker, for God's sake, tell me what's happened.'

'She's heard some unpleasant news too abruptly.'

Fanny struggled to speak. 'Please don't ask me,' she stammered. 'I don't want to be alone tonight and I've been on my knees to Parker begging him to stay with me. He refuses.'

'Surely you're not going to leave her in this state?' said Harriette indignantly to Parker.

'I can't do anything for her. It's too late. In ten days' time I shall be the husband of another woman. My presence is only an irritant to her.'

'Fanny, darling Fanny, don't make yourself miserable over this brute!'

'You won't cheer me up by abusing the father of my child,' groaned Fanny.

'Come to bed, Fanny dear,' said Harriette, taking her sister by the hand – it was burning.

'Yes, I shall be better in bed.'

Fanny was helped upstairs. Dry-eyed, she shivered and could not speak. Parker relented so far as to stay with her till one o'clock the next morning. Fanny stayed in bed for two days and felt better on the third. She asked for all news of Parker's marriage to be kept from her. She forced herself to go into society as usual but, whenever she walked fast or hurried upstairs, her lips turned blue; she was convinced she had a bad heart. A man she had turned down brought her not only the details of Parker's wedding but a piece of the wedding cake, an act of spite which prostrated her. Formerly humorous and cheerful, she was now sunk in gloom. Parker wrote that he would always visit her and his child. He even led her to believe he had made a marriage of convenience in order to get promotion in the army. But married he was, and not to Fanny. For women in her position, life was hard: she was penniless, a discarded mistress with four children, three of them bereaved by the death of their father.

Harriette left for Paris with Fanny's son George Woodcock, a fair, pink-faced boy, strong and active, with thick flaxen curls, dressed in a light blue jacket and trousers, with a small ruff round his throat. He did not know a word of French and swore he would take care not to learn it; he was afraid of picking it up by accident, like an infection. Harriette's mother and her sister Amy had come to Paris, where Amy entertained Lord Fife, Luttrell and Nugent, and Lord William Russell. Amy had found a shop that sold her favourite black pudding.

Julia, now nearing forty, could not contemplate leaving Napier, who was wealthy enough for her to overlook his long back and short legs. Meyler arrived and told Harriette that, never having had a Frenchwoman, he was going to try them for fun.

'A young man with £30,000 a year must try everything once,' he said, eyeing her with the intention of inflaming her jealousy. He needed the stimulus of cruelty; his pleasure was to torment her. Her pride protected her, but her heart was unsatisfied. She already regretted losing Worcester's loving kindness. She found young Frenchmen were interested only in young women – and Harriette was twenty-eight. In Paris, at last she went to parties, balls and masquerades – without success.

'We really hated each other, and yet sheer jealousy kept us together,' she writes. 'Meyler had no mind, no romance about him. His person was charming; but that won't do, even with gentlemanlike manners, for one's everyday companion … He who suited me was married,' adds Harriette sadly.

She soon decided to revenge herself on Meyler with his friend Lord Ebrington[4], whom she had met before she knew Meyler. She called on Meyler at his house as he was dressing to go out and threatened Meyler that if he persisted in going to the Duke of Devonshire's ball and leaving her alone, she would go to Lord Ebrington's 'and make love to him'.

'I'm sure you wouldn't leave me for Ebrington, handsome as he is,' said Meyler.

'Yes, I will, and this very night, if he's to be found, and you refuse to come home with me.'

Meyler sneered that even if Harriette were to 'invite Ebrington to your bed he wouldn't come to you'. Harriette accepted this gibe as a challenge. In accordance with her custom, she wrote to Ebrington offering to visit him at ten o'clock that evening. He came instead to her[5].

He was good in bed, the more welcome since Meyler's latest whim was to torment Harriette by arousing her and then refusing her sexual satisfaction. Ebrington was handsome and his manners, gentle and graceful, reminded her of Ponsonby's; the faithless Ponsonby was always her measure of what a man should be. She confessed to Ebrington the reason she had summoned him. Ebrington told her politely that he would have come in whatever circumstances. She found him soothing and delightful. In her own words:

> … it was impossible to avoid drawing comparisons by no means favourable to Meyler, who, though perfectly graceful and gentlemanlike, was far from well-read, and, as for conversation, he seldom spoke at all. Moreover, at this instant, I had reason to believe the provoking little reptile was actually in the arms of some frail, very frail, French woman.

Next morning, relaxed and satisfied, as they were drinking their breakfast chocolate in Harriette's luxurious dressing room, Harriette said to Ebrington: 'How was it that you paid me so little attention when I was young and pretty?'

'You were just another good-looking girl. We met only by accident, after all. Since then, I've heard of nothing but Harriette Wilson wherever I went; I couldn't help wondering what it was that Ponsonby and Worcester had found so charming.'

'You monster!' protested Harriette, stretching like a cat in the morning sunshine.

'Never mind, dear Harry,' said Ebrington, kissing her nose, 'I love you dearly after last night.'

'And I like you twice as well as I did six or seven years ago,' she retorted.

'Very complimentary to us both,' said Ebrington. 'In fact, you're now exactly what I've always liked. In the old days you were too shy for my taste.'

'Me? *Shy?*'

'I would have been thrilled if you had sent for me just because you fancied me. Nothing feels so good as having inspired an attractive woman with an irresistible desire to make me her lover. I remember a young widow, just the sort of woman I like; had a devil of a time getting her to agree to a private meeting. In the end, she came into my chariot and I took her to the end of a secluded lane at the back of her father's house. She said how wonderful it was to be alone with me at last. I've never forgotten how good she made me feel.'

He stayed till after two, promising to return that evening. Meyler arrived half an hour later and, as was always the case after he had been harsh and spiteful, was all smiles and tenderness. He told her he had been sleeping with as many Frenchwomen as he could find, but now he found them disgusting, and he was more in love than ever, he said, with Harriette: 'I was dying to see you, to kiss you, to ask your forgiveness on my knees last night: but it was too late, your house was shut up, and I didn't dare disturb you.'

'You'll never disturb me again,' said Harriette quietly.

'What do you mean?'

'I've seen Lord Ebrington.'

'Oh, when we passed your house in my barouche?'

'I'm not so platonic as that! No, I sent for him. You told me that if I did, he wouldn't come. What do you think of that now?'

Meyler trembled from head to foot.

'The suspense is killing me,' he said.

'I'll tell you if you promise not to beat me,' said Harriette, knowing his propensity towards violence under the guise of passionate love.

'Rubbish! Come on, tell me the truth, don't torture me.'

'Why not? You're not sorry for hurting me yesterday.'

'I was sorry, you know, after I'd left you.'

'Fat lot of use that was to me! I like variety, too, and I'm sure you'll congratulate me on my good taste when I tell you that Lord Ebrington slept here with me last night, and he can do it again tonight if he likes.'

Meyler burst into tears and begged her forgiveness for neglecting her. He pleaded with her to send Ebrington away and 'give me one more trial'. Harriette had picked up the habit, from Meyler's friends, of calling him 'little Meyler', though he was of normal medium height and well proportioned. 'But then,' writes Harriette, 'the expression of his features possessed that soft style of beauty which would have been suitable to a woman.' Harriette was always a sucker for male good looks of a feminine cast, in the then current fashion.

He stayed till after eight o'clock without his dinner, refusing alike to eat and to leave Harriette. At nine, she was expecting the return of Ebrington, but fasting and fretting had made Meyler seriously unwell. Finally, she said she would not turn him out of the room to make way for another man. She scribbled a few lines of apology to Lord Ebrington and handed it to the maid, asking her to carry the note down to the porter's lodge to be delivered to his lordship as soon as he came. Meyler, who throve on quarrels, was all joy and wild rapture. He wanted her to swear never to see or speak to Ebrington again. He said nothing stimulated him like a rival. But Harriette bore him a grudge for consorting with the lowest of women and would make no promises. Ebrington seemed at least to respect and love her; he was handsome, accomplished and thirty-one; this made him three years older than Harriette, while 'little Meyler' was much younger, almost a contemporary of Worcester. Both Meyler and Ebrington continued to call and to sit glaring at each other.

Lord Alvanley, insouciant aristocrat, who ate cold apricot tart every day

Fanny wrote to say that Parker took an interest in his daughter, little Louisa, and had visited twice. Fanny added: 'Brummell's sun, they say, is setting, which, you'll answer, was the story long ago; but since that, I'm told Brummell won £20,000, that is too now gone, and he is greatly embarrassed. Poor Lord Alvanley they say is just in the same plight.'

The story was this: Brummell, Alvanley and Worcester agreed to raise a loan of £30,000 on their joint securities. Brummell having made Worcester believe that he was at least competent to pay the interest on the debt, the money was raised and the responsibility for payment fell on the unfortunate Duke of Beaufort, Brummell and Alvanley being insolvent. Meyler was furious when he heard, on Worcester's behalf and on his own, for he had lent Brummell £7,000, believing he could be trusted. Although Alvanley had lent him pornographic books in the past, Meyler never spoke to Alvanley again and exposed Brummell at White's Club, which earned him the name of 'dandy-killer'. Meyler admitted that Alvanley's fraud was less serious than Brummell's in that Alvanley was capable of paying the interest. Alvanley sneered at Meyler, calling him 'a damned Methodistical grocer'. Harriette adds that Brummell, on his last legs as far as London was concerned, made his way to about a dozen former acquaintances, most of whom had already given him money. He said to them all: 'Play has been the ruin of me: I now throw myself on your compassion, being in a wretched plight; I've been led into such scrapes as oblige[6] me to leave London at a moment's notice, and I haven't a guinea to pay post-horses.'

Many of them gave him £50 notes. One of them first expostulated with the beau and asked what excuse he could offer for having already obtained such large sums from people who knew so little of him.

'Why,' said Brummell, 'haven't I called you Dick, Tom and John, you rogues? Wasn't that worth it to you? But for me, do you fancy or flatter yourselves that you'd ever have been seen picking your teeth in Lady Foley's box, or the Duchess of Rutland's?' Brummell shortly afterwards left for Calais[7]. Alvanley eventually inherited a fortune and paid all his own debts, amounting to £55,000.

Napier's passion for Julia continued to increase, said Fanny's letter, but 'why does he with his £20,000 a year suffer her to be so shockingly distressed? On the very day you left England, Julia had an execution on her house and the whole of her furniture was seized ... if he had really loved her, he surely would have immediately paid her debts, which do not amount to £1,000, as well as ordered her upholsterer to new-furnish her house.' Julia had followed Napier to Melton Mowbray to ask for money, but 'would you believe it? Julia has returned with merely cash or credit enough to procure little elegant necessaries for Napier's dressing room, and, for the rest, her drawing room is covered with a piece of green baize, and in lieu of all her beautiful little knick-knacks and elegant furniture, she has two chairs, an old second-hand sofa, and a scanty yellow cotton curtain. Her own bed was not seized. It is now the only creditable piece of furniture in the house of Napier's adored mistress, one of the richest commoners in England, who is the father of her infant … '

Harriette had hardly finished reading her letter when Lord Ebrington came and complained: 'You have behaved very badly to me.'

Harriette pleaded it was not her fault. She was separating from Meyler, she said.

'But he comes to see you just the same,' retorted Ebrington.

Harriette said Meyler's violent temper and indifferent health had to be taken into consideration; besides, he would not be staying long in France and it was unfair to upset him by allowing him to find Ebrington with her. She did not menton that Meyler paid the rent of her house as well as that of his own across the way. Ebrington, being proud, concealed his disappointment. She refused to tell him which theatre she was going to that evening, in case his visit to her private box should irritate Meyler. Harriette tells us: 'I still felt something like affection for him [Meyler], although I could never speak to him, or think of him, without getting into a passion.' She told Lord Ebrington, meanwhile, that he reminded her of her adored Lord Ponsonby. She stuck, though, to her 'little sugar baker' – and to his £30,000 a year. However, as long as Lord Ebrington hung around Harriette, Meyler was a delight to be with; as soon as Ebrington seemed to cool, Meyler left off being amiable and became actively unpleasant. He sneered: 'Ebrington got tired of you.'

Harriette said that if Meyler persisted in quarrelling with her, they would have to part. Sometimes, the spoiled, peevish boy would swear that he was so devoted to her that he would never marry; at other times he would say fidelity was not in his nature. He taunted her for having had previous lovers, saying he could neither respect nor like her. Yet still mutual sexual attraction bound them together, as in an unhappy marriage. Harriette lost her appetite for food and grew thin and depressed. He accused her of pining for Ebrington and staying with him only because 'I am so much richer'. This shaft struck home and put Harriette in such a rage that Meyler pretended to pass it off as a joke and left to dress for dinner.

Harriette promptly wrote to Ebrington, who came at once, showing delight at being reinstated. He stayed so long she was compelled to offer him dinner, although he was on his way to a dinner party elsewhere. Ebrington admitted that his heart was cold, though his passions were strong. His extreme gentleness appeared, though, most appealing after Meyler's roughness and morbid irritability. Harriette could not get Ebrington out of the house; he stayed another delightful night, leaving at three the next afternoon.

As soon as Lord Ebrington's carriage had gone, in popped the 'MP and sugar-baker', ghostly pale. His hands were icy cold.

'I saw Ebrington's cabriolet[8] and couldn't face going out to dinner. I waited to see him leave.' He made a scene and Harriette lost patience. 'For heaven's sake leave me alone!' she cried.

Meyler said he would go back to London and implored her not to let him see Ebrington visit. Harriette concluded that Meyler loved riding and good claret better than any woman. She began to fall in love with Ebrington's mind as well as his body. Both gave her pleasure in ways she had forgotten, dominated as she had been by Meyler's perversity. Meyler may have lived hard because he knew his time was limited; he had the transparent skin of a consumptive. She had found in Ebrington a companion suited to her in tastes and in age. Always she was moved and stirred by manly beauty. Ebrington resembled the actor John Philip Kemble, with features 'even more delicately turned'. He was a connoisseur of pictures and statues and an enthusiastic admirer of Napoleon, to whom he said he had some idea of paying a visit at Elba, an ambition he achieved, since in 1823 a pamphlet was published under the title *Memorandum of Two Conversations between Viscount Ebrington and the Emperor Napoleon at Portoferraio, December 1814*. A model English nobleman, he could put on a freezing reserve which mortified Harriette. His hauteur and satirical outlook made her feel inferior. He was with grand friends who were impatient to move on to Italy, and went. She decided he was naturally selfish. The possibility that she might have been guilty of selfishness herself never entered her head. She still pined for Ponsonby and ached because he was married. With her history, her chances of finding true love were slim.

Next day before she was out of bed Meyler called, looking sickly and complaining of digestive trouble that had plagued him for nearly a week. He announced that Paris did not agree with him and declared that his nerves would never allow him to live with a woman again. He held out his fashionably small, white hand; its delicate beauty and his melancholy mood moved Harriette towards liking him once more. Her mood changed, however, when he said men were more satisfactory friends than women, and that hunting was the only thing he was not tired of. He moved in with her for his last few days in Paris, where they slept in the same room but in separate beds. Their relationship had as many final appearances as a prima donna. Julia's version of events seems plausible; she says the split occurred in London. Meyler was planning to leave town:

Meyler at the opera asked Harriette to go home with him. She said she wanted to stay for the ballet.

'If that be the case, then to your friends I leave you, and I shall set off in an hour.'

Sir Harry Mildmay came in and she told him. After the curtain fell, she accepted Sir Harry's offer to set her down from his own carriage; and away they went … they proceeded to the Key, then a well-known brothel in Chandos Street, and supped and retired.

Mr Meyler ... went home about four in the morning, where he found no bird in the nest, but on the drawing-room table, a note from his faithful valet, whom he had ordered to have an eye on all Harriette's operations, to acquaint him, that he had watched and housed the parties at the Key; where he was on guard, near the door, to continue the pursuit, in case they should reappear after a bottle of champaign [*sic*], and was soon joined by his friend Harry Dyer, the Northampton buck, and they proceeded to discuss the affair, and the bottle, with all due hilarity. A £50 note induced the night-waiter to point out the room where the lovers were ... and the door was forced.

Harriette and Harry woke to see Meyler, Dyer and the valet armed with pokers in the middle of the room – Mildmay sprang out of bed in his shirt and Harriette jumped bolt upright ... [9].

Harriette was wearing nothing at all and the sight of his mistress in bed with another man let Meyler off any financial obligation towards her. Meyler 'had long suspected Harriette of inconstancy and therefore bore no enmity to his friend Sir Harry ... He well knew Sir Harry was not the seducer, and he ultimately behaved to his quondam mistress with a generosity few would have practised[10]'. He gave Harriette the furniture but stopped her allowance. Meyler, says Julia, wrote to Mildmay: 'When her desires are satisfied, she will cuckold you as she has done me.' Harriette had lost a protector with £30,000 a year. What was to be done? She took to tippling champagne and came out in a rash. Meyler was to die suddenly on 3 March 1818 at the age of twenty-six, leaving no will.

Once more unsupported, Harriette consulted her legal adviser, Henry Brougham MP, about her income from the Duke of Beaufort, which she had forfeited by writing to Worcester. Brougham, a distinguished lawyer and later England's Lord Chancellor, advised her to take the claim to court. Later she blackmailed Brougham about his adulterous relations with her.

During her stay in Paris, she was introduced to Lord Herbert, another man who struck her with his beauty. She asked if it were true that he was married to the sister of the Duke Spinelli. He answered angrily: 'Marry a damned Italian, old enough to be my mother? She answered my purposes while I was there, and we kept the intrigue going at the risk of both our lives – only place we could meet was the garden. The very night her husband died I made a bet that I could enjoy her as usual; won it, too.'

Harriette was disgusted at this coarseness, unsoftened by wit or humour: 'Not that I love a saint, but prefer what is luxuriously sly and quiet.' Quite.

One day when Harriette was driving up the Champs Elysées towards the Bois de Boulogne, the Duke of Wellington galloped past her carriage, then turned about.

'I thought it was you,' he said, 'and I'm glad to see you looking so beautiful. I'll come and see you. How long have you been in Paris? When may I come? Where do you live? How far are you going?'

'Which question do you want answered first?'

'I want to know where you live.'

'At 35 Rue de la Paix.'

'And may I pay you a visit?'

'Whenever you like.'

'I'll come tonight at eight o'clock. Will that suit you?'

'Yes.'

He was punctual and arrived in a grand carriage. He was covered with military decorations, ribbons, bows and stars.

'The ladies here tell me you make a bad hand at ambassadorship,' said Harriette.

'How so?'

'Why, the other day you wrote to ask a lady of rank if you might visit her *à cheval*; what does that mean, pray?' asked Harriette

'In boots, you foolish creature! What else could it mean?'

'The lady thought it just possible that the great "Villainton", being an extraordinary man, might propose to enter her drawing room on horseback, as being the most warrior-like mode of attacking her heart.'

'You little fool,' said Wellington, grabbing her for a rough kiss.

Napoleon had escaped from Elba and the English were hurrying away from France. Harriette's mother and Amy decided to stay, unalarmed. Harriette, having finally parted from Meyler, could not afford to stay, and she wanted to see Fanny, whowas still lodging with Julia. She went back to London. It was summer 1815.

Notes to Chapter Twelve

1. Page 144: The Russian emperor was so popular that crowds rushed forward to kiss his horse.

2. Page 144: Mentioned by name in Bulwer-Lytton's novel, *Pelham*, Chapter 32.

3. Page 148: Harriette says she spoke to Byron, but her account of their conversation lacks her usual ring of authenticity and is frankly dull. Harriette claims they discussed Lady Caroline Lamb's novel *Glenarvon*, not published till two years later. Julia doubts that Harriette ever met Byron, though she certainly wrote to him. Her letters survive among the Byron papers.

4. Page 145: Viscount Ebrington (1783-1861) was MP for Barnstaple 1801-7 and in 1841 became the second Earl Fortescue of Castle Hill. He was Viceroy of Ireland 1839-41 and Lord Steward of the Household to Queen Victoria 1841-50. He took an Oxford degree, and became a Fellow of the Royal Society in 1817. He married the same year, but his wife died ten years later.

5. Page 148: Despite her protestations that she was faithful to one lover at a time, she avenged herself on Richard Meyler with Lord Ebrington as she had avenged herself on Fred Lamb with the Marquis of Lorne.

6. Page 151: The pronunciation 'obleege' was now avoided as vulgar, having been condemned by Lord Chesterfield.

7. Page 151: Brummell left England in 1816. Harriet, Lady Granville wrote from St Omer on 27 February 1824:

Both Calais and this place are peopled with English, slight sinners and heavy debtors, the needy and the greedy. Berkeley Craven, who is settled at Calais ... says Mr Brummell ... enters into all the little gossip of the place ...

8. Page 152: Cabriolet, a light carriage with two wheels.

9. Page 154: *Confessions*, p276-7. In one version of the famous anecdote of Brummell asking - when snubbed by the Prince of Wales - 'Who's your fat friend?', Sir Harry Mildmay was present.

John Cam Hobhouse, Lord Broughton, friend of Byron, wrote in his diary (16 February 1840):

Met Sir Harry Mildmay, whom I had not seen for more than twenty years, and scarcely recognized the gay and handsome young Lothario whose follies made so much noise in my younger days. He is now fat and overgrown, with no pretensions to good looks. But he is lively and talkative ... and has many agreeable stories to tell' (*Recollections of a Long Life*, vol 5, p250).

10. Page 154: *Confessions*, 279.

13

HARD TIMES

Harriette got back to London late in the evening and was immediately visited by Lord Frederick Bentinck, as amusing as ever. Next morning she visited Fanny, bringing Fanny's boy, young George Woodcock, who on arriving in Paris a few months earlier had refused to learn their 'wretched lingo'. Now he had forgotten his English and answered everybody in French.

Prince Esterhazy[1], an old acquaintance, called. He spoke English with a German accent and usually carried a riding whip instead of the stick favoured by other dandies. Harriette asked him the purpose of his visit, reminding him that a begging letter she had sent him had remained unanswered. He gave her a £10 note and said: 'I want to meet some interesting young ladies.' He did not mean anyone, he said, at all common or vulgar, naturally; perhaps Harriette could give a party in 'this pretty, delightful cottage, and invite me to pay court to any young lady of your acquaintance — perhaps your sister?'

Harriette, faced with this blatant suggestion, reproached Esterhazy as a married man plotting to cause misery to an innocent girl. We wonder whether, at this point, she regarded her own career as one freely chosen or as 'misery'; she was nearly thirty, with neither husband nor lover.

'There are many girls who decide to fall,' said the roué, with a grin. 'All I want is that, when you see them going down, you'll give them — uh — a *gentle* push.' He took hold of her by the shoulders as an illustration.

Harriette declined to injure other women and told him she had tried to give Sophia a helping hand after her seduction by Lord Deerhurst[2]. If she came across a friendless girl who had been seduced and abandoned, said Harriette, she might present such a person to the Prince.

'Perhaps I might make some sort of settlement on her,' he said doubtfully. 'But, mind, she must be very young, very pretty, and *almost* innocent.'

'But you have the most beautiful wife in Europe!' cried Harriette.

A wife was altogether different, he said. 'I can't possibly stop now; I have to meet His Majesty at this very hour. Tell me the best time to find you and I'll come often. In the meantime, please write. You shall see me very soon.'

He hurried away, returning two days later, in a wet, muddy overcoat, as Harriette was about to eat her dinner. He stood in front of the fire, rudely blocking the warmth from his hostess and even more rudely keeping his hat on.

'I'm disappointed in you,' said he. 'It's high time I heard from you.'

'Take your hat off, Prince,' said Harriette, always touchy about disrespect.

'I never take it off,' was the brusque reply. 'I behave no differently to the first duchess in the land. It's my way and I'm not going to alter it; I'm too old to change. I saw two lovely sisters walking with their mothers today; their waists no bigger than that —' (making a circle with his hands). 'I followed them home. Do please get to know them —'

'Please leave my house,' said Harriette icily. 'Or at any rate, take off your hat and let me see the fire!'

The 'princely representative of imperial dignity, morality, disinterestedness and humanity' – in Harriette's own words – who wished to employ her as procuress, refused to do either. Eventually, disgruntled, he left.

Harriette heard from Fanny that Worcester was making up to a Frenchwoman who looked like Harriette and who had fallen seriously in love with him. But he was impotent with her and on the fourth futile night the lady had called him a fumbler and kicked him out of bed.

Lord Ebrington called on Harriette after his return from Italy and Elba. He declared he found Harriette delightful, but did not offer to pay her rent[3]. Amy was still in Paris, her married lover having left her, and she was making up to the Comte de Greffulhe, an ugly banker of Dutch origin, naturalised as a Frenchman and now a peer, with a fortune of £6 million sterling, but she had no success. Harriette was in debt and applied to the Duke of Argyll, who ignored her plea. She wrote to Byron, who sent her £50 from Ravenna. Restlessly she moved back to London, and tried her luck with former lovers, all of whom refused to help her.

One day Fanny, who had never left England, called as Harriette was dressing to go out. Harriette found this beloved sister sitting by the window, her head resting on her hand, looking pensive.

'My dear Fanny, what's the matter? Why didn't you come upstairs to me?'

Fanny laid a hand on her heart.

'I feel a weight here,' she said. 'It's not just depression; there's something not right here. I feel sick and faint.'

'A drive in Hyde Park will do you good,' said Harriette, and soon they were seated in the carriage. Turning down Baker Street, they glimpsed Colonel Parker, who showed no sign of having recognized them. Fanny was greatly agitated.

'I daresay he's only just come to town and intends to call and see his child,' said Harriette, hoping to soothe her. They drove up and down the park[4] and Fanny did her best to exchange greetings with the men who flocked round them. But after a brief while she complained again of sickness and a feeling of tightness round her heart. She asked to be taken home to Hertford Street, Mayfair[5]. She insisted her illness was not serious and asked Harriette to pick her up and take her out again the following day. Harriette did so and was stepping out of her carriage at Fanny's door, when Lord 'Red Herrings' Yarmouth came running downstairs from her apartment.

'Don't get out, Harriette,' he said, 'or you'll lose time. Go and get a surgeon at once – I was going myself. Fanny is very ill, and her physician has prescribed blood-letting, as soon as possible.'

Harriette found the surgeon and brought him home with her. Fanny was suffering from violent palpitations and assured Harriette that bleeding would do her good. Drawing Lord Yarmouth aside, Harriette asked him if he thought Fanny would get better. He did not think so.

'Pooh!' said Harriette, making light of her anxiety, 'Many people have palpitations and recover perfectly.'

Lord Yarmouth said gravely that he was afraid Fanny's heart was diseased. He had straw laid outside her door to soften the clip-clop of horse traffic. Her decline was rapid; within three weeks of the drive round Hyde Park, Fanny knew she was dying, and asked for her body to be examined after death in the hope of benefiting others. Only once did she mention Colonel Parker, calling her sister to her bedside at midnight and imploring Harriette not to be angry with him.

'It's true, you've written to tell him I'm ill and he doesn't come. It must be because he doesn't realize how ill I am,' said Fanny pathetically. Parker never appeared, not even to see their daughter, Louisa, but Lord Yarmouth visited, and acted kindly. Asking Fanny if there was anything she wanted, and being told she would like some eau-de-Cologne to cool her burning temples, instead of sending a groom, he galloped to town and back himself. He arranged for Fanny to be moved, at her own request, from Julia's home to Queen's Buildings in Brompton, then a country village with a garden, which cheered her up as she was carried through it. Amy and Harriette both spent much of their time in Paris avoiding creditors but, according to Harriette, they shared the nursing with Sophia.

Wistfully Fanny said she was happier dying where she was than in Julia's back room – perhaps they had already fallen out? 'I believe the view from the room above is beautiful, but I shall never see it,' said Fanny sadly.

Harriette opened the shutters, letting in the scent of honeysuckle. The last rays of the setting sun fell on Fanny's pale, beautiful face. It was a lovely June evening after a thunderstorm. Fanny asked her sister to raise her head so she could see the sunset one last time and Harriette cradled it and kissed her. Cold sweat stood on Fanny's forehead. Harriette watched her drink goat's milk. Harriette says Fanny implored Harriette to pray for her. Fanny crossed her hands on her breast and suppressed her groans. Her eyes raised to heaven, she looked 'like a martyr, severe in virtue and almost masculine fortitude'. With a convulsive effort, Fanny pressed her sister to her heart.

'May the Almighty for ever bless you,' said Fanny, falling asleep. The expression of agony was replaced by the calm smile of a sleeping child. Her breathing grew shorter and her heart stopped. Harriette says Fanny 'was my only friend on earth: I had no sister but her.'

'Frances Parker', aged thirty-three, was buried in Kensington churchyard in the summer of 1815. Her tombstone was moved when the old church of St Mary Abbot was demolished some forty years after her death. Three months later Harriette's beloved mother died, aged fifty-five, and Harriette's own fragile health broke down. 'There was nothing on earth, not even Fanny nor Lord Ponsonby, I ever loved, as I loved my mother,' she writes. Lady Berwick did not visit her dying mother, but sent baskets of fruit from the garden.

Harriette had in fact four other sisters living. Julia's version of events owes less than Harriette's to literary models. She says 'the deathbed of Fanny was dreadful. She screamed to live and had no hope of a blessed hereafter'. Julia says Harriette was in Paris at the time, though Harriette seems to have crossed the Channel fairly often:

> Fanny had, during Colonel Parker's absence in Spain, quite forgotten herself and intrigued with several men for money. Night after night she might be seen in the saloons of the theatres, arm in arm with Harriette, who went thither to procure money by the same means; she had led Fanny into those habits of thoughtless extravagance which finally proved her ruin, as it was the cause of Colonel Parker abandoning her and taking away the children ... he watched her at Drury Lane theatre, whence she and Harriette set off in a hackney coach and proceeded to a house of ill-fame ... Fanny had none of those fine feelings – hers were all blunted by depraved habits and intemperance ... [Parker's marriage took place] three years after Fanny's imprudence had laid her in a premature grave ... Colonel Parker [gave] her £50 a year ... [6]

According to Julia, Fanny was first kept by George Cooke the tragedian, who had a 'kind heart under a rude exterior. Both drank and lived hard'. Fanny used to sing and he grew jealous, threatening to cut out her tongue; he did scar her face. Fanny, writes Julia, was an alcoholic who walked the streets and had been treated in a Lock hospital[7] for venereal disease.

Harriette gives a touching account of a last meeting with Julia before the latter's supposed death[8]. A grieving Napier tells Harriette that he had his mistress laid out in state, with wax candles burning round her coffin for a fortnight; he had paid half her debts. Then, Harriette says, Napier began to make advances to Harriette herself.

Amy was still in touch with Luttrell and Nugent in Paris, where she was doing her best to convince the natives that black pudding was a rare English delicacy. She still cherished hopes of marrying the Comte de Greffulhe;

however, he resisted. As Gronow puts it, Amy was eventually married 'to a harpist of very doubtful character'. His name was Nicholas Robert Charles Bochsa, son of a composer. Bochsa was court musician to Napoleon and, after the Restoration, to Louis XVIII. He married a daughter of the Marquis Ducrest, brother of the celebrated writer and educator Madame de Genlis. Deeply in debt, Bochsa forged cheques and documents, using famous names, including the Duke of Wellington. In 1817 he fled to England, but was sentenced in his absence to twelve years' hard labour, branding and a four thousand franc fine. He married Amy bigamously at St George's, Hanover Square, in 1818. He became musical director at the King's Theatre and, after the Royal Academy of Music was founded in 1818, he was appointed Professor of the Harp. His success was shortlived, as in 1826 a letter to a musical paper, the *Harmonicon*, accused him of being a bigamist, robber, forger and runaway galley-slave. When these attacks were reprinted in the *Sunday Monitor* and the *Examiner*, Bochsa sued them for libel and won. But the scandal pushed him into a forced resignation from his Royal Academy post in 1827. However, he continued a successful career as a performer.

Amy may have been dead when in 1839 he ran away with a singer, Lady Bishop, wife of Sir Henry Bishop the composer, who sang professionally under the name of Madame Anna Bishop. The couple toured Europe – taking care to avoid France – America and Australia, where he died in 1856. The Australians gave him a celebrity's funeral.

Harriette's glory days were over. The Graces were no more, Fanny being dead and Julia buried in obscurity. Harriette was arrested for debt. She wrote various letters (often undated) to Byron from 64 rue Neuve des Petits Champs, and he occasionally sent her money, though according to her own account reminding her of her 'humble station' and of his own 'rank and talents'. In one letter to him she hoped that in twenty years' time they would take a pinch of snuff together ' … and as you watch me in my little pointed cap, *spectacles*, bony ankles and thread stockings, stirring up and tasting my *pot au feu*, you'll imagine Ponsonby's, Worcester's and Argyle's Angelick *Harriette* … '

Although Harriette had never pretended any friendship to Brummell, in his days of triumph or of disgrace, curiosity drove her to ask for him as she passed through Calais on her way to Paris, in or after 1816. His French language-teacher told Harriette that Brummell was charming and had a perfect French accent, which was amazing, since he had never previously learned any French. Harriette made the Beau a hasty visit and was received by his valet, one who could have served Brummell in the days of his glory – powdered, formal and well dressed. He said Brummell was shaving. Harriette was about to leave her card, but the valet told her that Brummell often received people while shaving or being shaved. He was grooming himself for the second time that day. Brummell received her in his dressing gown, still shaving with the tiniest razor

Harriette had ever seen. He looked plumper than in the old days, but fresh-faced; it did not appear that his disgrace had affected him.

Play, he said, had been the ruin of them all.

'Whom do you include in your all?'

He said there had been 'a rot in White's Club'.

'I've heard all about your tricks in London,' said Harriette.

Brummell laughed and said he sought only French society, as there was nothing more ridiculous than going abroad and then mixing only with English people.

'Don't you find Calais a melancholy residence?'

'Not at all. I draw, read, study French and —'

'Play with that dirty French dog,' interrupted Harriette.

He laughed and encouraged the animal to play tricks. His table was covered with seals, chains, snuff-boxes and watches – presents, he said, from Lady Jersey[9] and various other ladies of high rank.

'The only talent I could ever discover in this beau,' writes Harriette, 'was of having well-fashioned the character of a gentleman, and proved himself a tolerably good actor'[10]. Always a snob herself, she tells us that a certain unnatural stiffness of manner betrayed the parvenu. His wig, she adds cattily, was convincing. Men after the turn of the century had begun to wear their own hair, but Brummell was bald. He lived till 1840, having been offered a sinecure as British consul at Caen meanwhile. In 1837 he suffered two strokes, becoming senile and incontinent, and was taken into a charitable asylum run by nuns.

Back in London, Harriette was followed by a man in the street. He was tall and handsome, with a military moustache. Harriette had always been fond of military men. 'Zounds,' one of her lovers is said to have exclaimed after meeting her with two private soldiers, 'if the girl has no virtue she ought to have some decent pride about her; and all this time I've been keeping two huge guardsmen instead of a mistress.' Her new man was William Henry Rochfort, who had a distinctly shaky claim to the Earldom of Belvidere, an Irish peerage which had become extinct in 1814. Rochfort is the romantic hero of Harriette's novel *Paris Lions and London Tigers* as Mr Bellfield; Belfield was the Earl of Belvidere's second title. Rochfort was altogether a dodgy character and called himself Colonel, though of no particular regiment.

Julia, referring to Matthew Lewis's novel *The Monk*, called him 'the Rugantino of the Brothel', and tells us he was 'for a very short time a Colonel in some unknown corps of South American Independents, and a full Cornet [a very junior officer] in Lincoln Stanhope's regiment, the 17th dragoons ... ' Rochfort was currently in the Rules – or boundaries – of the Fleet Prison for debt. Prisoners were allowed to wander out upon payment of fees. Like that other debtors' prison the Marshalsea – to be immortalized by Charles Dickens in *Little Dorrit* – the Fleet had a fairly relaxed regime.

Harriette became totally infatuated with Rochfort, despite continued ill-treatment. She made a Fleet marriage, which was not legally binding, and could not hold him for long. Fleet marriages were ceremonies performed in the prison by broken-down clergymen who, being without resources or churches, were unafraid of the £100 fine for conducting a clandestine marriage. With neither banns nor licence to validate them, such marriages were of dubious standing. When Harriette was summoned by the Marlborough Street magistrates in February 1829, charged with assaulting her French maid, Rochfort was asked if he was her husband. He denied it, though admitting she had been known as Madame Rochfort for some time in France.

Harriette was in love with her soldier. She managed somehow to pay his debts and release him from confinement. He showed his gratitude by repeated infidelities, and several times left her to live with other women. Once she wrote to him, enclosing a lock of her hair, and waited for him to come back. A knock on the door made her heart jump. It was not Rochfort but a dirty little boy who gave her a letter and ran away. Rochfort's new girl wrote returning the hair, which he did not want; she had rolled it in the dirt and stamped on it. Rochfort came back to Harriette and they lived together again, mainly in Paris to avoid creditors. Calling herself Madame Rochfort, Harriette still had enough influence to get her letters carried in the diplomatic bag until its use by unauthorised persons was abolished by the British ambassador, Lord Granville Leveson-Gower, who, as Worcester's uncle and the man who had been marched about London, had at least two reasons for disapproving of Harriette.

Rochfort, frustrated child of a bastard son, had a grudge against the world in general and against the arrogant, insouciant aristocracy in particular. He felt cheated. He needed money for drink and women. His [common-law] wife had a saleable commodity: her charms might have faded, but now instead of love for sale she had memories that could be turned into cash by a two-pronged attack. Let the lords who had slept with her before making conventional marriages pay up or be made to squirm! He set her on to blackmail them.

Harriette turned and bit the hands that had fed her. Henry Brougham, England's foremost advocate, had given her legal advice. His bill, like others, had been paid in kind. He was an ugly man, with a bulbous turned-up nose and was known to hate his wife, a widow when he married her in 1819. Harriette wrote to him on July 14 [1824] ' ... of course for Rochfort's sake I can't talk of you as a lover ... ' As for Leinster, she told Brougham she intended to make him laughed at. Later in the year, she wrote to Brougham from Warwick Court, Holborn: ' ... This is a desperate effort to live by my wits since I cannot make up my mind to [be] an unfaithful wife ... old Wellington is writing us threatening letters about prosecution, hanging etc, which we laugh at. Two noble Lords have preferred buying themselves out quietly or rather a Lord and a Duke.' She adds that 'Marquis Graham, Lord F Conyngham and Lord R Manners' had all paid up. Handsome Lord Francis Conyngham of the Household Cavalry was later Lord Mountcharles and Marquis of Conyngham.

Many others must have bought her silence. Fred Lamb, as we have seen, threatened to sue but did nothing. The *Memoirs* became a best-seller, making £10,000 in the first year, a hefty sum. People bought them, talked excitedly about them, and refused to let their daughters read them. Newspaper cartoons showed Harriette and her lovers, one with a defiant gentleman saying, '£200 indeed! What would my wife say?'

Paris fashion in 1826

On 31 July [1827] Harriette wrote to Brougham: ' … rather than see my husband want *I will expose all your vices, follies, confessions, etc* … you treated me in all (but *paying me*) with all the cold disrespect due to a common prostitute. You did not even show towards me the feelings of a gentleman – for though you cut your wife on a Sunday … to intrigue with me, whose *poverty* rather than her *will* consented, you not only *offered me nothing* but was only induced to send me £10 by a decided *threat* after kinder means had failed.' She adds she has the accompanying letter to prove it and hard necessity might force her to publish it, together with others. On 16 December she wrote that there was no reason 'why *you* should have your *adultery and love letters concealed* for nothing while your friends pay for concealment of theirs. I once thought you had some regard for me … ' and threatened to send Mrs Brougham a copy of the letter if she did not receive an annuity of £40: 'I will accept £30 a year, if tendered directly and gratefully,' she conceded. A postscript says: ' … as you came to intrigue with me on a Sunday morning *after* your love of me was gone, it must have been your usual way of passing the Sabbath … ' Brougham sent her £20. She nagged for an annuity of £40 and asked Brougham to give her husband a job. Brougham did not comply.

Julia says the letters were composed not by Harriette but by Rochfort, who left Harriette in 1831 for another man's wife and died in 1852. However, Harriette was a dangerous woman. The King was still trying to buy back the compromising letters from Lady Conyngham to Lord Ponsonby. In 1832 Harriette complained to Brougham, now Lord Chancellor and ennobled as Baron Brougham and Vaux, that she had been forced to sell her piano to prevent its being seized for non-payment of rent, and says she wants 'somebody to love and like and look up to … and there's nobody but you', adding a request for another £40.

Her last surviving letter is dated November 1832 – she rarely put the year on her letters – from Pimlico, to Bulwer-Lytton, whom she had pursued with fan-letters since his first success with *Pelham* in 1828, saying she was desperately ill. She died at 3 Draycott Place, Chelsea, aged fifty-nine, on 10 March 1845.

Let the mortally offended Julia have the last word, with her pen portrait of Harriette:

Imagine to yourself a little woman in a black beaver hat and long grey cloak. No tightening at the waist to show the figure of the wearer, nor any ornament whatever. Her figure, at a short distance, might not inaptly be compared to a milestone with a carter's hat resting on its summit. Her once little feet are now covered with list [cloth] shoes, to defend them from attacks of a desultory gout, which she has suffered long in both extremities. Her face … swollen. [Her rosy colour has disappeared] and in its place appears a kind of dingy lilac, which spreads all over her … countenance, and appears burnt into her lips. The crow's feet are wide spreading beneath her eyes; which, though sunken, still gleam with faded lustre through her long dark eyelashes. She bears the remains of what was once superlatively lovely – the wreck of the angel's visage is yet to be seen; it looks interesting in decay – not the decay brought on by age and infirmity, but beauty hurried away prematurely, from the practices of a licentious and dissolute life; such is the once celebrated Miss Dubochet, alias Wilson [11].

Notes to Chapter Thirteen

1. Page 158: Prince Pál Antal Esterhazy (1786-1866), diplomat of Hungarian extraction. In 1806 he was secretary of the embassy in London and in 1807 in Paris. As Austrian ambassador 1815–42, he took a leading part in the negotiations after the wars of 1813–15. He was actually the same age as Harriette. He had married Thérèse, daughter of Charles, Prince of Thurn and Taxis, in 1812; her mother was a cousin of George IV.

2. Page 158: If Sophia did fall, it was, as we have seen, on her feet.

3. Page 159: Julia was convinced that Ebrington paid Harriette for sexual services (*Confessions*, p348).

4. Page 159: According to Gronow (p57), early in the nineteenth century 'pretty horse-breakers [expensive prostitutes] would not have dared show themselves in Hyde Park; nor did you see any of the lower or middle classes of London intruding themselves in regions which, with a sort of tacit understanding, were then given up exclusively to persons of rank and fashion.' However, Gronow's *Reminiscences* are sometimes rose-tinted. Harriette's visits to the Park seem to have been exercises in self-advertisement - she speaks herself of looking there for 'conquests'. Harriet, Lady Granville writes in a letter (25 August 1820) of 'fye-fyes' in the smart part of the Park among the gentry and nobility.

5. Page 159: We may assume that Fanny was among Lord Yarmouth's many mistresses, at this time if not earlier.

6. Page 161: *Confessions*, p296.

7. Page 161: Lock hospital, hospital for venereal diseases.

8. Page 161: It was reading of her own imaginary deathbed and Napier's grief that aroused Julia's fury. She wrote her *Confessions* in a hurry immediately on reading Harriette's *Memoirs*.

9. Page 163: Lady Jersey was the mother of the Duchess of Argyll, Lady Ponsonby and Lady William Russell.

10. Page 163: Lord Glenbervie, staying in France after Waterloo, wrote:

> [My son] Fred, while walking in the garden about an hour ago, met Brummell, who as soon as he perceived him hung his head down and brushed by him. He is under a strong imputation of having, together with Lord Alvanley, swindled Lord Worcester into being security for them in a very large sum, and upon the discovery of the transaction Brummell left London suddenly (*Journal*, 8 August 1816).

Some years later, Greville visited Brummell:

> I had a long conversation with Brummell, and was moved by his account of his own distresses to write to the Duke of Wellington and ask him what he could do for him. I found him in his old lodging, dressing; some pretty pieces of old furniture in the room, an entire toilet [set of brushes] of silver, and a large green macaw perched on the back of a tattered silk chair with faded gilding; full of gaiety, impudence and misery (*Diary*, 6 March 1830).

11. Page 163: *Confessions*, p94.

APPENDIX

'Old Bombastes Furioso'

'Everybody knows' that the Duke of Wellington said to Harriette, when she sent him a blackmail letter: 'Publish and be damned!' But did he? Julia would seem to have started this rumour:

> I should like to know of Miss Wilson, if she did not send to the Duke of Wellington for £300, threatening in case of non-compliance to write anathemas against his moral reputation; and if the Duke did not send her back her letter with 'write and be d—d' written in red ink on the back of it[1]?

What the Duke actually said, or wrote, and to whom, is not certain. He admitted to a close friend, Mrs Charles Arbuthnot, that he had known Harriette 'a great number of years ago', adding that he had never seen her since his marriage [to the Honourable Catherine Dorothea Sarah Pakenham, known as Kitty, second daughter of Edward Michael, second Baron Longford, on 10 April 1806] but 'had frequently given her money when she wrote to beg for it'. In her *Diary* Mrs Arbuthnot describes Harriette as a 'common street walker' who 'turned into ridicule the Duke of Wellington, who she claimed as one of her lovers … ' in 'an infamous book'; the Duke said she had 'offered to leave him out of her book if he would pay. This of course he refused to do and has never given her a farthing since she threatened him'[2].

Writing to her husband, Mrs Arbuthnot described the *Memoirs* as 'great nonsense … What she says of the Duke is so ridiculous and so unlike him that I should doubt her knowing him except in his generosity in giving her money[3]'. The suspicious diarist Greville was convinced that Mrs Arbuthnot was herself the Duke's mistress, but it seems unlikely, though he was believed to be in love with her.

Elizabeth Longford, in her biography[4] writes that the sum demanded of each of Harriette's lovers was £200 and that on 16 December 1824 Harriette's publisher Stockdale, not Harriette herself, wrote to the Duke as follows:

24 Opera Colonnade

MY LORD DUKE

In Harriette Wilson's Memoirs, which I am about to publish, are various anecdotes of your Grace which it would be most desirable to withhold, at least such is my opinion. I have stopped the Press for the moment; but as the publication will take place next week, little delay can necessarily take place.

This letter is supposed to be the one on which the Duke wrote 'Publish and be damned!' in 'flaming red ink'[5]. Lady Longford is, however, sceptical of 'this cherished tradition': the letter is in Apsley House, 'Number 1, London', the Duke's home. There is nothing on the back of the letter and the Duke, although he scrawled replies on letters received 'sometimes used pencil instead of dark ink, but never red ink'. She says that a second letter from Opera Colonnade shows 'that the Duke had indeed told Stockdale to go to hell and take Harriette with him'. Dated 28 December 1824, it reads:

Mr Stockdale was certainly not aware that the Duke of Wellington had been threatened by Harriette Wilson now Rochfort …

and continues to threaten, mentioning sums of £5,000 and 'twice that sum'.

Harriette herself writes that the Duke threatened to prosecute if 'such trash' were published, a word to which she took exception. She reminded him that he had 'bribed Mrs Porter over and over again' and that 'old frights like himself, who could not be contented with amiable wives, but must run about to old procuresses, bribing them to decoy young girls … ought to pay us for … our secrecy.' She says: ' … Wellington sends the ungentle hint to my publisher, of hanging me, beautiful, adored and adorable me, on whom he had so often hung! … Is it thus he would immortalize me? … goodbye, old Bombastes Furioso.'

Notes to Appendix

1. Page 169: *Confessions*, p 213.

2. Page 169: *Diary* , 19 February 1825.

3. Page 169: Quoted in E A Smith, *Wellington and the Arbuthnots*, p64.

4. Page 169: Longford, *Wellington*, p109.

5. Page 170: *Wellington*, p110.

BIBLIOGRAPHY

AIRLIE, Mabel, Countess of   *Lady Palmerston and Her Times* (1922)

ALBEMARLE, George Earl of   *Fifty Years of My Life* (1876)

ANGLESEY, Marquis of (ed)   *The Capel Letters, 1814–17* (1955)

ARGYLL, Duke of (ed)   *Intimate Society Letters of the Eighteenth Century* (1910)

ASPINALL, A (ed)   *Three Early Nineteenth-Century Diaries* (1952)

BAMFORD, Francis, and Duke of Wellington (eds)
                               The Journal of Mrs Arbuthnot 1820–32

BERKELEY, Grantley F   *My Life and Recollections* (1865–6)

BESSBOROUGH, Earl of, and A Aspinall (eds)
                               Lady Bessborough and Her Family Circle (1940)

BICKLEY, Francis (ed)   *Diaries of Sylvester Douglas, Lord Glenbervie* (1928)

BLANCH, Lesley   *The Game of Hearts* (1957)

BOURNE, Kenneth   *The Blackmailing of the Chancellor* (1975)

BULWER-LYTTON, Edward   *Pelham* (1828)

BURY, Lady Charlotte   *Memoirs of the Times of George IV* (1838–9)

CASTLE, Egerton (ed)   *The Jerningham Letters 1780–1843* (1896)

FRASER, Flora   *The Unruly Queen* (1996)

GRONOW, R H   *Reminiscences and Recollections* (1862)

GROSVENOR MYER, Valerie   *Obstinate Heart* (1997)

HARRISON, Wilmot (ed)   *Thomas Moore Anecdotes* (1899)

ILCHESTER, Countess of, and Lord Stavordale (eds)   *The Life and Letters of Lady Sarah Lennox 1745–1826* (1901)

ILCHESTER, Earl of (ed)   *Journal of Elizabeth, Lady Holland* (1908)

JOHNSTONE, Julia   *Confessions* (1825)

KEPPEL, Sonia   *The Sovereign Lady* (1974)

LE FAYE, Deirdre (ed)   *Jane Austen's Letters* (1995)

LEVESON-GOWER, F (ed)   *Letters of Harriette, Countess Granville 1810–45* (1894)

LONGFORD, Elizabeth   *Wellington* (1992 edn)

MAXWELL, Sir Herbert (ed)   *The Creevey Papers* (1903)

PONSONBY, Sir John   *The Ponsonby Family* (1929)

PRIESTLEY, J B   *The Prince of Pleasure* (1969)

RAIKES, Thomas   *Journal 1831–47* (1856)

SMITH, E A   *Wellington and the Arbuthnots* (1994)

TENENBAUM, Samuel   *The Incredible Beau Brummell* (1952)

THIRKELL, Angela   *The Fortunes of Harriette* (1936)

VICKERY, Amanda   *The Gentleman's Daughter* (1998)

WALKER, John   *Pronouncing Dictionary* (1809)

WILSON, Harriette   *Clara Gazul* (1830)
Memoirs (1825, and various editions)
Paris Lions and London Tigers (1825)

WILSON, Philip Whitwell (ed)   *The Greville Diary* (1927)

WYNDHAM, Honourable Mrs Hugh (ed) *Correspondence of Sarah Spencer, Lady Lyttelton 1787–1870* (1912)

INDEX